HOW GOOD IS YOUR CHILD'S SCHOOL?

ABOUT THE AUTHOR

Before retirement the author served for thirty-six years as a teacher, principal, and superintendent in both elementary and secondary school districts. He also participated in numerous Middlestates Evaluations of other elementary and secondary school districts where he gained valuable experience in the art of evaluating the strengths and weaknesses of public school education.

The author has a BA degree from Montclair State College, a MA degree from Columbia University, and has done extensive postgraduate work beyond his master's degree at Rutger's University and other colleges.

He has published six juvenile novels and numerous plays in *Plays Magazine.*

HOW GOOD IS
YOUR CHILD'S SCHOOL?

Everything You Should Know About The School
System Before You Buy That New House

By

ELBERT M. HOPPENSTEDT

CHARLES C THOMAS • PUBLISHER
Springfield • Illinois • U.S.A.

Published and Distributed Throughout the World by

CHARLES C THOMAS • PUBLISHER
2600 South First Street
Springfield, Illinois 62794-9265

© *1989 by* CHARLES C THOMAS • PUBLISHER

ISBN 0-398-05627-7

Library of Congress Catalog Card Number: 89-37465

With **THOMAS BOOKS** *careful attention is given to all details of manufacturing
and design. It is the Publisher's desire to present books that are satisfactory as to their
physical qualities and artistic possibilities and appropriate for their particular use.*
THOMAS BOOKS *will be true to those laws of quality that assure a good name
and good will.*

Printed in the United States of America
SC-R-3

Library of Congress Cataloging-in-Publication Data
Hoppenstedt, Elbert M.
 How good is your child's school? : everything you should know
about the school system before you buy that new house / by Elbert M.
Hoppenstedt.
  p. cm.
 ISBN 0-398-05627-7
 1. Public schools—United States—Evaluation. I. Title.
LA217.H65 1989
371'.01'0973—dc20   89-37465
                                                         CIP

INTRODUCTION

Are you one of those parents who can't decide where to purchase a home because you don't know whether the school system in the municipality is the kind you want to send your children to? If you are, you're not alone. Ask any real estate agent and he'll tell you that the first question he is asked by a prospective house-buyer is, "How good are the schools?"

Never before in the history of American Education have the public, the government, and parents paid such close attention to how the nation's schools are performing. Parents and government officials are giving the schools a close, hard look, and in many cases they don't like what they find.

Fifty years ago it was unheard of for a parent to criticize his child's education. When Johnny's mother was summoned to the school for a conference with a principal or teacher, she entered the hallowed halls with a great deal of trepidation and reverence. Whatever the principal or teacher would say to her would be Gospel Truth. If Johnny wasn't paying attention; if he was failing; if he was a discipline problem, there was no question but that Johnny was at fault. The school did not make mistakes. The Pope and the public schools were infallible. And fifty years ago they probably were. At least, as closely as any human institution can be.

What happened? In the late forties, after World War II a group of educators (college professors who had never taught in a public school and who were given the task of educating the teachers and administrators who would be teaching the children of the postwar baby boom) preached that the old ways of teaching had to go. They were too didactic, too dreary, dry, and dull. What were needed were new innovative programs that challenged America's youth and made learning interesting.

Nothing wrong with that, with the intent, that is. But when it came to putting this philosophy into practice, a number of serious mistakes were made. Phonics had to go. Sight reading would take its place. Strict discipline was out the window. A student needed to be relaxed, to be himself, or real learning and creativity couldn't take place.

v

And rote learning, that evil of all evils, was out the schoolroom window. As with most "revolutions," whether they be in government or industry or in this case, education, the theories were carried to extremes. Had there been a happy marriage of the old and some of the more innovative programs of the new, probably American education would not be in the mess it's in today.

Not only are the parents up in arms but the business community as well. For years industry had been donating large sums of money in an attempt to induce the schools to improve student achievement. But these monies have been, for the most part, "poured down the drain." Now industry is taking a new approach: In Chicago, businessmen and philanthropists have become so disgusted with the public schools that they have decided to start an elementary school of their own. The funds for this school have been forthcoming from sixteen companies including Sears Roebuck, MacDonald's, and United Airlines. The school has been set up so that its results can be compared fairly with the public school's—the same per pupil spending, teacher pay, pupil-teacher ratio *and,* most importantly, in the type of student that is enrolled. (The school is located in Chicago's slum area.) The 150 students were picked by lot from 2000 applicants, all from black or Hispanic low-income families.

Teachers at this corporate-community school will visit each student in his home and encourage parents to become involved in their child's education and in the running of the school.

Fortunately, there are also a number of public schools who are making serious efforts to raise their students' achievement. It's interesting to note that a preponderance of these schools are turning back to the traditional practices of our forefathers. However, it isn't easy to retrain teachers and administrators, and even more difficult to retrieve the kind of discipline the schools of our grandparents were familiar with and expected.

As parents we have the responsibility to make sure that the schools our children are attending are offering top quality education. But how to make a rational judgment? Do we listen to the neighbor next door who has just had a run-in with the school principal because her son has cut twelve days of school since the term began and tells you it's not the boy's fault because his teacher doesn't teach, he just passes out work sheets and doesn't bother to grade them? And you ask politely, "From whom did she get this information?" And she tells you, from her son, of course—where else?

This is the problem most parents face. It's difficult to evaluate their child's school because most of what they know about it is hearsay—from their children, neighbors, the clerk in the grocery store. Furthermore, they have no reliable and comprehensive criteria with which to make an evaluation.

This book will provide you with a detailed, evaluative process. It will, at the conclusion of each segment, offer a simple, easy-to-follow rating guide.

The information needed to complete the evaluations can be obtained in a number of different ways:

(1) *Interviews.* Those matters which pertain to the operation and supervision of the entire school system can be answered by making an appointment and conferring with the superintendent of schools.

To obtain answers to question relative to the operation, curriculum, discipline, or any other matter pertaining to a particular school building, meet with a principal or vice-principal. If the matter at hand has to do with discipline, see the vice-principal, because in the typical school today, a vice principal usually is in charge of behavioral problems, truancy, cutting classes, drug-related problems, and attendance-keeping.

Most schools today, both elementary and secondary, have a guidance department, and it is here you should go for questions pertaining to your child's achievement, or lack of it.

Health questions can be answered by the school nurse, a position required by law in most states.

2. *Attend Board of Education meetings.* A lot can be learned about the school system's philosophy of education and how it is carried out by attending these meetings. At these meetings you will hear reports made to the board by various agencies of the system.

The superintendent will make requests of the board—for new programs, for revisions, for texts, for equipment, and for alterations to the physical plants. In most states, he will present to the board nominations for new faculty members and other professional staff. He will outline their qualifications and why he has selected them. From this you can get an excellent insight into the type of people he is bringing into the school system and his thinking behind the selection.

Usually the superintendent compiles the annual budget. Copies are supplied to the public in attendance. By listening to the superintendent's explanation of each line item, you can get an excellent idea of where he is placing his emphasis as to how your tax dollars are to be spent. There should be a good balance of funds for programs versus funds for such things as night-lighting of the football field and computers for his office.

3. *Observing classes.* There was a time when the classroom was off limits to outsiders. But today, with the increasing pressures being felt from the press, from organizations, and from parents, most schools will permit parental visits if arrangements are made ahead of time. It's usually a good idea when asking to visit a classroom to present a specific objective as your reason for making the request. Examples: Your child says he never has any homework; you want to verify the fact that he does. You've heard so much about the "new math"—you want to learn more about it. You're interested in seeing how reading is taught.

When you make the actual visit, however, you will not limit yourself to observing only the objective you stated as your reason for coming. You will be observing every detail of the teacher's interaction with her or his class to get an accurate picture of the total effectiveness of her or his teaching. Here are some things you should look for:

A. The rapport between the teacher and the class. Is there a feeling of mutual respect? Is the teacher at ease before the children? Do *all* the children participate enthusiastically?

B. What is the condition of the room—is it neat and orderly, but also clearly evident that the books, globes, maps, blackboard, audiovisual equipment, etc. are being used by the students?

C. Are all the students attentive? Is there evidence of students' work displayed about the room. (This is particularly important in elementary grades.)

D. Is student behavior conducive to good learning?

E. How adept is the teacher at classroom management?
(In grades kindergarten through fourth or fifth grade more than one activity should be going on at the same time for much of the day to take care of individual differences.)

In other grades, observe how the teacher passes out papers; collects homework; goes over written work and corrects it; records grades; manages attendance taking; takes care of individual requests for leaving the room for such purposes as to see the nurse, meet with a guidance counselor, go to the boys' or girls' room; handles classroom discussions; makes assignments; controls student blackboard participation, etc. All these activities should be done as quickly and as efficiently as possible with a minimum of confusion and a maximum of clarity.

(For a more detailed discussion and explanation of the above points, refer to Chapter Six.)

4. *Examine courses of study.* A course of study is an outline of what

should be taught in a particular subject or grade level, the objectives to be obtained, what measurements are to be used to determine if the objectives have been met, the texts and other materials and audiovisual aids that are to be available for the teacher's use, as well as other community resources that can be utilized.

5. *Examine texts, the physical plant, equipment, supplies, etc.*

The above topics will be explored in greater detail in the appropriate chapters to follow.

Armed with the above avenues of approach, you, as a concerned and educated parent, can now begin the process of evaluating your child's school. By the time you have finished reading this book and have completed the Rating Guides at the end of each segment, you will have a comprehensive, accurate picture of what your child's school is like. You will probably find that there are areas of strength and areas of weakness. What you must do, if that be the case, is to determine whether the weaknesses are in important areas of your child's education, and if so, take measures to have them corrected.

To assist you in interpreting each of the graphs you will have constructed upon completion of this book, the following procedures may prove helpful:

1. Draw a vertical line from the top of the graph to the bottom half-way between the 2 and the 3. This will help you separate those entries which are below average from those which are above.

2. Add up the numbers for each entry. Divide the sum by the number of entries to obtain an average for the section. Or you can add the numbers for the entries to the *left* of the vertical line, figure their average, and then compare this average with that of the items to the *right* of the vertical line.

3. Circle the x's of all entries which you consider most pertinent to your particular school situation. Compare the number and importance of those to the left of the vertical line with those to the right.

4. Upon completing the book, go back to each of the evaluations and write down the entries which you circled under #3, those which fall far to the left of the vertical line. Arrange them in the order which you feel to be most critical insofar as your school district is concerned. Use this list when seeking changes from your board of education or top-ranking officials.

CONTENTS

HOW GOOD IS YOUR CHILD'S SCHOOL?

Chapter One

ORGANIZATION

District-Wide Organization. The organization of the public schools in this country varies slightly from state to state. In general it consists of a board of education, which may be appointed or elected; a chief school administrator, usually referred to as the superintendent of schools; principals for each of the separate schools; vice-principals, if the school enrollment warrants it; and, in the high schools, a director of guidance and various department heads who are usually in charge of the staff, curriculum, and regulation of one or more subject matter areas.

The Board of Education's responsibility is to set policy and to consider and act upon recommendations brought before it by the superintendent of schools. Unfortunately, this is not always the case, and many school systems have gotten into trouble because individual board members, or the board as a whole, takes over certain functions ordinarily reserved for the professional staff. There have been accounts of board members evaluating teachers, spying on principals and teachers, taking charge of the janitorial staff, running the cafeteria, reprimanding students, and in one case, directing traffic in the student parking lot every afternoon at dismissal because his son's car had been damaged and according to him "the administration had done nothing to find out who the culprit was."

When board members interfere with the running of the schools, havoc usually follows. If the interference centers on the teaching staff, the local teachers' union (or teachers' association if affiliated with the National Education Association) will probably file a grievance. In most states, when this action occurs, the Board of Education acts as the first hearing body. If it cannot resolve the problem, then the state supplies mediators to hear the case.

The public, and parents in particular, should have their ears to the ground for any such problems existing within their school system. Why? Because no other problem can filter down more quickly and affect the degree of learning going on in the classrooms more profoundly than interference from a board of education.

Political Boundaries of School Districts. To illustrate the best and the worst system of political subdivisions set up by the various states, let's examine two systems—New Jersey and Florida.

In Florida there is *one* board of education for each of the various counties. Each county has one superintendent of schools. All of the schools in that county are managed, financed, and regulated by a single board of education through a single administrator.

In New Jersey, on the other hand, each municipality, no matter how small, is a separate entity. It has its own board of education, its own superintendent of schools. It makes policy for the schools within its jurisdiction and is financed by local taxes and, to some extent, by state aid. And to make matters worse, in some instances there is a separate board of education and administrative staff for the elementary schools and for the secondary schools within the same district. In one instance, two municipalities each has its own elementary district and sends its students to a regional high school district which has its own board of education and own administration and competes with the elementary district for tax dollars. In one county in the state of New Jersey there are over thirty separate autonomous districts within one county.

What are the advantages and disadvantages of the two different systems, New Jersey's and Florida's?

Let's do this by comparing New Jersey's system with the one in operation in Florida. Proponents of New Jersey's system suggest that having separate school districts in each municipality allows for home rule and permits educators to fashion their curriculum to the needs of their students. But others, who favor a change to a county wide district, argue that there really are no great differences between the needs of students in one district with those in another, particularly when the districts are situated close to one another geographically. Besides, they further state, individual needs of different geographic areas can be resolved just as effectively by a county administration as they can by a local board of education by allowing each school building within its jurisdiction greater autonomy in drawing up its educational objectives and courses of study.

Now let's take a look at the disadvantages. First, from a viewpoint of cost efficiency, in the example cited above in which a county had over thirty separate independent districts, it's not difficult to enumerate the unnecessary duplication of staff and personnel. At the top level we have over thirty superintendents of schools, each drawing at least $50,000 a year in salary for a total of over a million and a half dollars. This doesn't include assistant superintendents, curriculum specialists, all of the personnel that make up thirty separate financial managers and secretaries who are responsible directly to the various boards of education, or the many heads of departments which oversee such agencies as pupil transportation, atypical students, cafeterias and food management, janitorial services, and maintenance of buildings and grounds.

Besides saving considerable sums of money by consolidating all of these various departments and personnel under one county board of education, additional savings are realized though a single system of purchasing. These include such items as textbooks, educational supplies and equipment, food, janitorial supplies and equipment, school buses, and in the purchase of land and the erection of school buildings. Anyone who is familiar with purchasing procedures knows that by buying in volume considerable savings are made and better quality products are supplied.

Although proponents of the present system in operation in New Jersey maintain that local educators are better able to meet the needs of their students because they are closer to the problems and better understand the needs, there are others who disagree. "We have visited states where the educational division is by county," they argue. "We have studied this system in depth, and we are convinced that a single county-wide school district actually does a better job of taking care of the individual needs of all the students. Under this system greater resources are available as a result of consolidation; more trained personnel can be hired to supervise and administer to these needs. In New Jersey, rich districts perhaps equal the performance of Florida's system, but in the poorer districts, where the greatest needs usually exist, pupils are being shortchanged. "In Florida, the wealth is divided more evenly and concentrated where the needs are greatest."

But by far the greatest advantage of a county educational system is the more coherent, more efficient educational program it will invariably produce.

In New Jersey, as mentioned above, two towns may have separate elementary districts and both send their ninth, tenth, eleventh and twelfth grades to a common regional high school district. Under such an arrangement, it becomes extremely difficult to coordinate the curricula of these schools. The two elementary districts each develop its own courses of study; the high school is then required to assimilate these students and produce a course of study which takes into account the diverse needs of the two elementary district pupils.

Not too far away geographically from these three school districts is another combination of autonomous districts consisting of *four* elementary districts and a regional high school to which these districts send their pupils.

In both of these situations the administrators of the elementary sending districts and the regional high school have made an heroic effort to standardize their curricula, but the problems with such a task are overwhelming, and the amount of time needed to do a thorough job is not available.

Furthermore, whenever plans for consolidating the curricula among the elementary school districts are submitted by the administrators to each of the local elementary district boards of education for approval, these boards invariably conclude that here again is another example of the regional high school district trying to impose its will on them.

Division by Grade Levels. School systems are organized in another way: by the grade levels contained within each building. Back before the turn of the century, all school systems had the first eight grades contained in the "grammar school" and the last four years in the high school. Around the nineteen-thirties, a number of school systems began to experiment with a new division of grades. They reasoned that seventh and eighth and possibly ninth graders didn't fit in well with the lower grades, and they were too young to be included in the high school years. Thus was born the junior high school, usually consisting of grades seven, eight and nine.

Since that time there have been two other combinations: the 6-2-4 plan and the 5-3-4 plan. Often the particular plan employed by a school system is determined by such factors as geographic distribution of students, minority distribution, transportation problems, hazardous road conditions, population densities, and a score of other reasons. However, it should be said that any of these plans—the 6-3-3, the 5-3-4 or the 6-2-4—are equally as effective and better than the 8-4 plan. Any plan which separates the middle-aged students from younger children is a good one.

Young adolescents are too immature in their behavior and in their needs to be placed with the older high school students, and too sophisticated to be in the same building with younger children. When they are with younger children there's a tendency for the older students to tease and harass the younger ones, and the younger children often mimic many of the behavioral patterns and offbeat language of the older ones.

Organization Within Each Building. Organization within an elementary school is rather simple; lower grades are assigned to rooms at one end of the building and upper grades to another. Separate assembly programs are conducted for the lower grades and for the upper grades. Kindergarten and primary classrooms are assigned near the "playground," while the upper grades use the athletic fields.

Curriculum-wise, an elementary school consists of three major levels—primary grades, intermediate grades, and upper grades.

The high school is a far more complex organization. Most high schools are scheduled for a seven-period day, each period lasting from forty-five minutes to an hour. A three- to five-minute passing time is allowed between periods, depending upon the size of the building and how long it takes for a student to move from one end to the other.

Some high schools schedule an average of one study period during each day; other schools have done away with the study hall because most students nowadays prefer to do their studying at home. As a result, study halls in many schools become a battleground between the teacher—who attempts to enforce quiet—and the students who would rather "rap" about what they did the night before and what's on tap for the coming weekend.

The physical arrangement of the classrooms and the special areas of a high school building play an important part in how successfully its program will function. When laying out plans for a modern high school, the architect must consider a number of requirements.

All offices should be centrally located: the central office, the guidance offices, the health suite, the principal's and vice principal's offices, and the attendance office.

The media center (library) should be close to the academic classrooms. The auto shop should be in the rear of the building, adjacent to parking and driveways and away from all academic classrooms. So should the wood shop, metal shop, print shop, and all other classrooms of the type which tend to be noisy.

The cafeteria, also used frequently as a meeting room or study hall, should be isolated from study rooms. Gymnasiums, too, should not be too close to the academic classrooms.

The auditorium is an important part of the school program, and also frequently serves the community at large. Often it is a separate building, or if that is not possible, is situated in a wing or is a projection from the

main building and is adjacent to the main entrance. This permits its use
by the community during the day when not required by the school.

Some means of isolating the auditorium from the rest of the building,
either by doors that can be locked, or a gate that can be pulled across the
corridor is a must whenever the facility is used at night. Restrooms
should be provided in this area for public use.

The band and choral rooms must be isolated and often soundproofed.

In most high schools academic subjects are placed in clusters of rooms
and a work room or office is located within the cluster for teachers to use
in planning their lessons and correcting papers during their "free period."
Science rooms should have an adjacent preparation room and a storage
room.

Preparing students' schedules at the beginning of each school year has
become an extremely intricate and difficult job. Without the use of a
computer, the task is almost insurmountable.

Whoever is in charge of student scheduling must consider the following limitations:

(1) Class size. He or she cannot schedule more students during one
period than the classroom will hold. For instance, if a chemistry lab has
twenty positions, and the computer places twenty-five students in the
class, the programmer must form another class. But now he is faced with
another problem: he will have only five students in the second class.

The problem may be resolved by shifting the class to another period
in the day when other students, who could not be programmed before,
can now be fitted into the new class time.

(2) Students' ability. More and more schools are scheduling students
homogeneously, particularly in such subjects as mathematics, English,
science, and sometimes social studies.

This homogeneous grouping permits the teacher to present his or her
material on a level that is more easily assimilated than it could be if the
class were heterogeneously grouped.

(3) Special needs. Students who are on a work-study program, for
example, must have all of their classes programmed during the morning
hours so they will be free to attend their jobs during the afternoon. The
hard of hearing may have to be placed in special sections for some of
their subjects. Many vocational programs are so scheduled that the
student has his academic studies in the morning and then goes to the
vocational area of the building for a full afternoon of uninterrupted
classes in the vocational field of his choice.

(4) Subjects which require double periods. Many times science laboratory experiments need more time than a single period permits. In such cases the programmer must so schedule these students that they have two periods together. In like manner, home economics classes may require a double period.

(5) Child development classes. Many high schools now have a program labeled "child care" or "child development" for juniors and seniors. During the latter part of the course, preschool children are transported to the high school so that these students may have "hands-on" training in the care and upbringing of young children.

These classes should be scheduled to meet at a time that is convenient for the parents of the young children and at a time when school buses are available for their transportation. The middle of the morning is the preferred time slot.

(6) Scheduling students for a lunch period is a real challenge to many school districts unless the school is small enough so that all students can eat at one time. Most school cafeterias cannot handle more than about four hundred students at one time (many of these students do not purchase school lunches, but will bring their food from home; some will bring their lunch and purchase milk).

The average time allotted for lunch in most high schools is one-half hour. In a school of 1200 or more students, three lunch periods are needed.

If class periods are three-quarters of an hour in length, dividing two of these periods into three lunch periods works out about right. A student goes to either first, second, or third lunch and has a class during the rest of the time, usually an extended period of one hour.

But for those students who have second lunch, the arrangement is far from satisfactory because the one-hour class period is broken in the middle with a lunch period. The student goes to the class for a half an hour, to lunch for the second half hour, and then back to the same class for the last half hour, not the best of arrangements.

For schools that have longer than forty-five minute periods during the day, the problem is exacerbated, for now the class time during the lunch break can be as long as an hour and a half.

Most educators agree that a class period this long is counterproductive. Students become restless and lose attention. As a result, some schools have used the time by adding a shorter period of about a half hour for clubs, extracurricular activities, homeroom, or short assembles.

Minority Distributions of Pupils. During the last thirty years much confusion has existed in the public schools of this nation because of Supreme Court decisions requiring that schools be balanced ethnically and racially. A great number of plans have been formulated to resolve the problems this mandate has caused. Busing nonwhite students to all white schools and vice versa has been the most popular solution. Other solutions have included the construction of new buildings in areas from where students from all racial groups could be drawn, rearrangement of the geographic areas assigned to different schools, and a combination of these three plans.

Opponents of the Supreme Court mandate have denounced integration of the schools to achieve racial balance and have insisted that when minority students are brought into white schools the quality of education is diminished. And if the white students are transported to the minority school, they insist, these students are provided with an inferior education.

While this may be true in a small number of cases, this author has found that *if the number of minority students is a small percentage compared to the host school, then the opposite is true* —the high caliber of the parent school will tend to accelerate the motivation and achievement of the minority students.

When white students are transferred to a minority school, one of two things is apt to take place if the number of students being transferred is significantly fewer than the number of students already enrolled in the school: (1) The white students will tend to isolate themselves from the others, and if they were superior students before the transfer, they will continue to be superior students. (2) A certain percentage of the white students will integrate with the existing student body and tend to operate on their level. (3) The existing student body may ostracize the white students. (4) The two groups may integrate without any problems.

Size: Student Enrollment. Is there an ideal size for a school? Most educators believe that there is a definite relationship between the size of a school and the ability of administrators to solve problems and increase student achievement.

A high school with a small enrollment is limited in the number and scope of courses that can be offered. On the other hand, too large a school population presents problems of management, discipline, scheduling, and overall control. The ideal high school enrollment is probably between 1200 and 1800.

Elementary schools fare better when they are small. Because classes in the elementary school are self-contained, there is no advantage curriculum-wise to large numbers of pupils. In a school district it is better to have a number of smaller elementary schools than fewer, larger ones. Best enrollment in an elementary school is probably between 300 and 800.

Homogeneous Grouping. Various types of homogeneous grouping have been used in the public schools for the past hundred years. Back in the days of the one room school house, a teacher, through necessity, had to divide her class into groups based on their ability or on their achievement level. Each group was then assigned work on its level, and the teacher would move from group to group to give them assistance and move them on to the next phase of work.

Since then schools have homogeneously grouped students for a variety of reasons: (1) to take care of the needs of the superior student, (2) to take care of the needs of the slow learner, (3) to take care of the needs of those with special problems, (4) to isolate those students who presented severe disciplinary problems, (5) on a temporary basis, to help those who needed remedial work in a particular subject.

Evaluation

Place an x for each entry to rate your child's school system. Then connect the x's with a continuous line to form a graph. 1 = low; 5 = high.

1 2 3 4 5

- My child's board of education sets policy and direction for its superintendent and does not interfere with the internal working of the schools.
- My state has a county-wide system of school districts.
- My child's school district is organized so that the middle school pupils are separated from the younger and older children.
- The high school in my school district has eliminated study halls because they are a waste of valuable time.
- The building housing the high school is well planned to separate various activities and avoid noise interference.
- The building housing the high school contains classrooms for college-bound courses, business courses, and vocational training.
- High school students' schedules are completed by the opening of school and contain few conflicts.
- Solutions to the Supreme Court decision for racial balance have brought about few problems in my school district.

                                                    1   2   3   4   5

- The elementary schools in my school district have enrollments within acceptable limits.
- The high schools in my school district have enrollments within acceptable limits.
- My school district uses homogeneous grouping to solve special problems.

Chapter Two

BUILDINGS AND GROUNDS

A board of education in the United States probably controls the greatest assets, in terms of dollars and cents, of any other municipal or county subdivision. In larger cities, the worth of the buildings and grounds of the school district can run into the billions of dollars.

Except for newly formed districts, the buildings controlled by a board of education vary in age and type of construction. Some of these older buildings go back to the turn of the century and are usually constructed with a large, formal entrance way in the front, large, high-ceilinged classrooms with ornate "tin" panels, and boys' and girls' rooms down in the basement (from which derived the standard pupil request, "can I go to the basement?").

These buildings were usually at least two stories in height. Often the stairwells were constructed of wood. The central office was situated immediately beyond the front entrance way.

Many of these older buildings have been modernized, and if they have, often serve as well as a modern building for an *elementary school*. But most often the cost of renovating such buildings exceeds the cost of tearing them down and erecting a more modern plant.

NATION'S SCHOOLS NOT AGING GRACEFULLY

Washington—More than 22,000 school buildings in the nation are inadequate and thirteen percent of those are structurally unsound, says a study released recently by the Education Writers Association.

The study found that one in four of the public school buildings in the United States need maintenance or major repairs, and are either overcrowded or obsolete.

Many also present environmental hazards.

Another third are, at best, "only adequate and because of growing enrollments and deferred maintenance could easily become inadequate," concluded the study which has been entitled "Wolves at the School-house Door."

One-fifth of the country's schoolhouses were built more than fifty years ago, the association said. Nearly two-thirds were built in the 1950's and 1960's.

If there is an older building still in use in your district, these are the alterations and improvements which *must* be made to bring it up to modern standards:

Heat. Most of these older buildings originally contained a coal burning furnace which supplied steam to free-standing radiators in each of the classrooms and hallways. The furnace and the entire system must be replaced. The simplest and usually the most efficient way of doing this is to place outside-vented electric heating-air conditioning units in each classroom with a thermostat that is individually controlled. These units also exchange a fixed, hourly volume of air as required by the state.

Lighting. Fluorescent lighting is the accepted type of illumination for the modern classroom. Some industrial arts shops may use mercury lamps. Each state publishes guidelines on the number of footcandles of light that must reach each pupil desk on the darkest days.

Electrical Rewiring. The electrical cable and control boxes must be completely replaced. The type of conduit used in these older building is now considered unsafe; mice and other rodents often gnaw through the insulation and cause short circuits. Furthermore, the high voltage requirements of the heating units and the new lighting fixtures necessitate much heavier cable.

Often the replacement of the wiring in these older buildings is the most difficult task of all. Exterior walls are usually thick concrete and brick and wires cannot be "snaked" through them. Yet much of the electrical needs are located on these outer walls.

Flooring. The wooden joists and floorboards must be replaced if the building is to be made less of a fire hazard. This can be a very costly renovation and in many instances makes the entire project impractical.

Windows. The windows in older school buildings were constructed of wood. Scores of coats of paint over the years may have made them inoperable. These windows should be replaced.

Stairwells. All stairwells must be made completely fireproof. Exit signs must be installed top and bottom. Most important of all, these stairwells must be isolated from the hallways above and below with fireproof doors.

Blackboards. Natural slate was used, some of which has probably shattered and chipped over the years, or so filled with chalk dust that it is no longer usable. It should be replaced with modern "greenboard."

Other, Minor Renovations. Boys' and girls' rooms, if possible, should be moved out of the basement. Water fountains should be modernized. Standardized clocks, containing an intercom system, should be installed. A gymnasium, and possibly an auditorium, should be added if they are not already included.

As stated above, these older renovated buildings could equal their modern counterparts if they were utilized as elementary schools. This distinction was stressed because the high schools built in the early part of this century just do not have the facilities required for a modern secondary institution.

A few of these deficiencies are (1) The lack of up-to-date science laboratories, (2) no classrooms for vocational or business training, (3) lack of space for teacher planning, (4) small gymnasiums without sufficient seating for spectators, (5) insufficient acreage for football, soccer, tennis, track, baseball, and other sports which are a part of the modern high school program (most older schools were built on small parcels of land), (6) no guidance area or nurse's suite.

Some districts have utilized portions of these older buildings and have attached additions to them. While this is a partial solution, these stopgap measures are not really the best answer, and many school districts find that after ten or twenty years they must tear down both the original structure and the additions and start from scratch.

When a new school building is in the planning stage, the architects and the educational authorities of the school district must take into consideration three important questions:

(1) How well will the building perform *functionally?*
(2) How well will the building perform *educationally?* and,
(3) How well will the building perform *maintenance-wise?*

The following paragraphs will discuss each of these questions.

How Well Will the Building Perform Functionally? This question asks the architects to design a building that is easy and cost-efficient to maintain. The type of materials that go into the building, for instance, must be durable and not require constant repair or refurbishing. Examples: A slate roof will last a lifetime; an asbestos shingle roof probably twenty or twenty-five years. A flat roof is forever leaking in one spot or another unless it is frequently recoated.

Terrazzo floors are expensive but they are much easier to keep clean than asphalt tile, and they last forever. How about the surfacing of the corridor walls? Students love to run their pencils along them as they walk to their next class. Ceramic tile is easily cleaned, painted cement block is not.

Where are the large mixers and other machines in the cafeteria kitchen to be located so that the workers can do their job more efficiently? Where will the dishwasher be placed so that it's convenient to where the students dispose of their soiled dishes and trays? How about the walk-in refrigerator? Should there be an exterior door for garbage disposal? Where should it be placed?

Where are the janitors' slop-sinks? Are they located along the halls at convenient locations? Are there sufficient electric outlets along the corridors and in the classrooms for the janitors to hook up a floor polisher and vacuum cleaner?

Hundreds of questions like these must be answered for every section of the building and for every activity that will take place to keep the building clean and in repair. Once the construction has commenced, change orders are very costly. And after the building is occupied and in service, changes usually are out of the question.

The architect must design a structure that can be maintained with a minimum of effort and expense and is so arranged that activities can be carried out expediently.

How Well Will the Building Perform Educationally? Many boards of education make two basic mistakes when planning the building of a new school.

First, they may tend to economize to the point where the educational program of the school will be in jeopardy for the life of the building. Such an error is often predicated upon the belief that the taxpayers will not support any larger, more efficient building (in states where school buildings are financed through local bond issues).

This belief is not often the truth. The public generally is not against the *size* of the building, but against "frills" and other unnecessary or costly options, such as swimming pools, spacious entry halls, or student "rap" rooms.

It is important to point out those areas where boards of education will often make cuts in a building in order to reduce the cost of the project, cuts which later may cost tenfold to correct through the erection of additions or alterations, or may not be correctable at all.

1. *Size of Auditorium and Gymnasium.* When planning a building, it is usually the practice to make projections on the number of students who will be attending the school for the following five or ten years. From

these projections, administrators determine what the student capacity of the building should be.

Therefore, an anticipated enrollment of one thousand requires at least a double gymnasium so that two classes can be participating at the same time. Double gyms usually have an electric powered folding door to separate the two areas.

But what frequently happens, particularly in school districts which have large areas of undeveloped land, is a sudden influx of housing developments and, as a result, far more students than were originally anticipated.

When planning a gymnasium's size, spectator seating must also be considered. While it is true that these bleachers can be folded up to take less room, nevertheless, considerable additional space must be provided for them.

Auditorium size should be determined by two factors: the size of the student body and the anticipated number of spectators which can be expected at plays and other performances put on for the public by the school. However, duplication within the school district is also something to be avoided; for instance, the elementary schools can use the high school facilities for all their public performances, and thus a combination cafeteria-assembly room will suffice for the elementary schools.

No school expects to seat its entire student body at one time in the auditorium. Two sessions are usually considered to be a good ratio of the number of seats in an auditorium compared to the total anticipated student body five or ten years down the line after the school has opened.

2. *Science Areas.* A very serious error made by many school districts in planning a new high school is not to allow for sufficient space in each of the special science rooms. A chemistry classroom, a physics classroom, or a biology classroom therefore, should consist of the following: A laboratory area of at least twenty-four stations, a separate area in the same room for lectures and classroom work with separate desks adapted to book work and writing, an office for the teachers who use the room, a preparation and supply room where the teachers may prepare demonstrations and experiments, and where shelves along the walls can hold the myriad of supplies used in a modern high school. This preparation room should contain water, electrical outlets, and gas burners, as should all of the student stations in the laboratory area.

Other science rooms, such as those in use for general science or earth science, can contain fewer of the essentials noted above.

3. *Shops, Home Economics, and Vocational Training.* These are expensive areas to build, and as a result the number and size of these rooms are often reduced to lower the cost of the building. However, this is usually false economy. Look for the following in these specialized rooms:

In the auto shop, which is usually part of the vocational training program, expect to see at least two lifts, plus a pit. There should be an extensive area for student work with workbenches and cabinets for tools. There should be a separate room for parts and supplies and an office for the teacher. At least two overhead doors should open to a large paved area where students can work on cars when the weather permits.

An exhaust system for the entire room is a must, as well as individual units that can be attached to all car exhausts whenever the engines are running. Recommended, too, is a separate room, away from the main work area, in which cars can be prepared for painting, painted, and left to dry. Here, too, students can work on collision damage.

The wood shop and the metal shop should contain the following: space for at least twelve benches (24 student positions) with ample space between each bench. Sufficient space for locating all power tools with at least an eight foot area around each machine which can be marked off with a red strip, beyond which no student goes while the machine is in operation.

A wood storage room for the wood shop and a smaller storage area for the metal shop is a necessity. Each of these rooms should have a teacher's work room and office. The wood shop should have an air tight, well ventilated room for spray painting.

The print shop should have a large area for offset presses, photo work and preparation of plates. Some print shops still feel the need for a letterpress and ample space should be provided for this. A paper cutter is a necessity.

Home Economics, now open to both boys and girls, requires at least two types of rooms, for cooking and related subjects, and for sewing. Most high schools also include a room for child development and related courses.

The number and type of courses possible in a vocational training program are endless. The criteria for selection must always focus on the *needs* of industry in the locality in which the school is located. In-depth studies are required long before the high school building is begun. Members of the industrial community, civic leaders, the general public and, of course, school officials should comprise the committee which presents its recommendations to the board of education.

When examining the vocational program in your school system, the best method for ascertaining its success is to speak with the management of all principal industrial and commercial enterprises in the immediate geographic area and ask them whether the vocational program is filling the needs for replacement of their trained employees.

4. *Business Education.* Here again, many planners of future high school buildings do not adequately anticipate the needs of the school. Again, rooms and adjacent service areas are often too small in square footage, or the number of rooms needed to adequately serve a well-rounded course of study, are lacking. Depending upon the size of the district, and the scope and type of businesses in the area for which the school must train workers, all or some of the following specialized classrooms should be included in the building:

(1) Typing rooms should include sufficient electrical outlets for each typing station. Overhead outlets have proved most efficient; those located on the floor, after a year or two of use, tend to become dislodged from constant movement of desks or student abuse, and also become clogged with dirt and dust.

(2) Computer training rooms are usually included under the jurisdiction of the business department, although in some schools the mathematics department has control. As long as time is divided equally between the two, which department has control is unimportant.

(3) Business education rooms are enlarged classrooms and do not require any special features.

(4) Stenography classes can usually be held in any regular classroom.

(5) The same is true with bookkeeping classes, as long as the room contains large-surfaced desks.

5. *Cafeteria.* The most serious error in planning a school's cafeteria is lack of adequate storage space and too small an area in the kitchen for the preparation and dispensing of food. Too few serving lines is another serious mistake. If lunch periods are limited to about thirty minutes, as they are in most high schools, students must be able to move through the serving lines quickly if they are to have sufficient time to eat without rushing.

In many schools which have too few serving facilities, there is usually a mad rush to get to the cafeteria at the close of the previous class and considerable safety problems can result.

6. *Lockers.* The general practice is to locate student lockers along the walls of corridors. While this arrangement causes obstruction in traffic

flow during changes of classes, it is the most economical location. Some schools, to solve the congestion problems, have located the lockers in special off-corridor rooms. But this solution also has its drawbacks. Such areas are difficult to supervise, and they too, tend to congest unless traffic flow in and out of the rooms is through separate doors.

7. *Stairways.* There has been much discussion on the merits of single-floor schools versus two or more stories. Usually the amount and cost of the land available determines which type of building to erect. However, there are many two-story buildings being built in the suburbs and country where land is relatively cheaper.

Proponents of the two-story school believe that by placing a second story on top of the first, considerable money is saved because the floor of the second story serves as the roof for the first. Advocates of the single story building argue that this saving is lost because of the space that is used for stairwells to the second floor.

Present-day schools are conscious of the needs for the handicapped, and a school with two or more stories requires an elevator which is another expense which limits the cost effectiveness of the multi-story building.

In most states the number and placement of stairwells is regulated by state guidelines. The number of students housed in the building and the distance from the farthest classroom are determining factors.

8. *Foreign Language.* The teaching of foreign languages in the modern high school requires a "language laboratory." More about the requirements of this room will be discussed in the next chapter, EQUIPMENT.

9. *Guidance and Health.* Out of ten schools with which this author is acquainted, eight have indicated that the guidance area was built with too few offices and, in general, too small an area to take care of the needs of the school after a few years in operation.

A guidance center should contain offices for each of the guidance counsellors, one for the guidance director, a conference room, an outer office, storage areas, and possibly an isolated, soundproofed room for testing. Planners should always anticipate that after a few years the building will contain more students than the capacity for which it was built, and therefore more guidance counsellors will be employed than had originally been planned for.

In the nurse's suite, many schools do not provide sufficient space for ill students to lie down while awaiting treatment or the arrivals of their parents. Usually, too, the examination room is too small and as a result becomes congested during physical examinations.

10. *Art.* A high school which expects to have a well-rounded program should contain the following facilities:

(1) A room devoted entirely to painting and drawing. It should contain storage areas which can be locked, and there should be a sufficient number of lockable bins in which each student may place his work during the time he is not in class. These locked bins are needed to prevent other students from mutilating or accidentally breaking or marring another student's work.

(2) A ceramics room which should contain an auxiliary room to house the kilns and supplies. This auxiliary room should be situated so that it can be easily controlled and monitored by the instructor.

(3) A crafts room which would be used for weaving, raffia work, paper mache, stained glass, wood carving, hot-wax cloth dyeing, and the scores of other hobbies currently popular.

11. *Music.* Two large rooms are required for a high school music program, one for instrumental music and the other for choral music. The instrumental music room should contain tiers or some other method to elevate the student players. Both of these rooms should be thoroughly soundproofed and should be located near the auditorium.

12. *Media Center.* It's unfortunate that architects and boards of education fail to include sufficient space for the media center when designing schools. They fail to realize that the media center is the hub of learning in today's school, and requires considerable space in order to carry out its functions.

Too many architects still think of the media center as solely a library, a place to stack books. The modern media center comprises a much broader concept; besides books and magazine a well-run media center will contain phonograph records, tapes, slides, video tapes, film strips, movies, picture collections, exhibits, and works of art.

To house all of these collections and to provide sufficient space for students to make use of them requires careful planning. In designing a library, of all the rooms in a school building, this is one area where it is better to overbuild than to skimp. It is usually not possible to expand a media center after the building is in use except through considerable expense or loss of classrooms on either side of the center.

A modern media center should contain sufficient space to stack all books, plus room for additional stacks should they be needed in the future. The media center should also contain private booths for viewing film strips or listening to tapes and records. There should be a large room for student research. The media specialist and·her assistants should have ample office and storage rooms.

13. *Janitorial.* A number of smaller rooms, located just off the corridors, each containing hot and cold running water and sufficient space for mops, brooms, and other equipment, is better than larger rooms less frequently placed throughout the building. A locker room for the janitorial help is needed, as well as showers and possibly a small lounge.

14. *Athletic Fields.* Five acres plus one additional acre for each one hundred students enrolled in the high school is a formula often used for determining the minimum amount of land required for a modern high school. Considering the importance that high school athletics plays in our society today, no high school can possibly get by without a football field with sufficient bleachers, a running track, shot put, high and broad jump pits, soccer field, tennis courts, baseball field, softball field, and a field hockey field.

Thirty or forty years ago girls participated in, perhaps, no more than two or three interscholastic sports. Today they take part in all the sports that boys do, save perhaps, football, and have in addition several of their own. For this reason, the acreage required in a modern high school increases as the years go by.

Most boards of education have been farsighted when acquiring land for secondary schools, particularly boards whose districts are situated in the suburbs or country where land is still available.

Most of the fourteen areas discussed above have pertained to the secondary school and do not always apply to elementary buildings.

Because the elementary school building is simpler in design and usage, boards of education are less likely to make serious errors in the design and arrangements of classrooms. There are, however, several areas that should be discussed:

1. *Sizes of Classrooms.* The kindergarten and preschool areas should be considerably larger than the classrooms built for the upper grades. Children in this age range require a good deal of space because their attention span is short, and the teacher is required to move the group to new activities.

A section of the room should be set aside for large, manipulative toys—rocking horses, small indoor slides and swings, tricycles and the like. Another section will be used for cooperative games; another for rest periods; another for hands-on toys like dolls, special educational puzzles and the like.

There also should be an area of tables and chairs where these children can crayon and paint and look at picture books.

Classrooms for older children should be designed to coincide with the school's philosophy of class size. However, experience has shown that many schools start out idealistically with small classes, but later must revise their estimates upwards. For this reason it is better to make upper-grade classrooms larger.

2. *Special Areas.* All elementary schools should provide space for guidance counselors, the nurse and medical advisor and dentist, a gymnasium, rooms for the faculty, teachers' lounge, offices for the principal and vice-principals, a lunchroom and kitchen, an assembly hall (which may be combined with the cafeteria or gymnasium), and the following outdoor facilities: swings, slides, sand boxes, and play areas for the younger children; a baseball field, a soccer field, track facilities, and several outdoor basketball backstops for the older classes. If the school district is in an area where football is a popular sport among the townspeople, a football field is also a necessity.

Evaluation

Place a x for each entry to rate your school system. Then connect the x's with a continuous line to form a graph. 1 = low; 5 = high.

1 2 3 4 5

- Older buildings in my school district have been modernized or demolished or used for purposes other than instruction.
- have examined school buildings erected within the past few years and find them to be well-planned functionally, educationally and maintenance-wise.
- High schools which have been built recently are adequate in the following areas: (To obtain the information needed to complete this section, interview the various heads of the departments or a principal or vice-principal).

    Auditorium

    Gymnasium

    Science rooms and labs

    Shops

    Vocational education

                                                        1 2 3 4 5

        Business education
        Cafeteria and kitchen
        Student lockers
        Foreign languages
        Guidance
        Health
        Art
        Media Center
        Music
        Janitorial services
        Athletic fields
•   Elementary schools have sufficient space for:
        Guidance
        Nurse
        Media center
        Playground and athletic facilities
•   All elementary schools contain:
        Offices for the principal and vice principals
        A gymnasium
        Cafeteria and kitchen
        An assembly hall (may be combined with cafeteria)
        Teachers' room

Chapter Three

EQUIPMENT

The contractor has completed his work and the board of education has formally accepted the new high school building. Now comes the momentous task of equipping the numerous classrooms, as well as the special educational and noneducational areas.

Needless to say the administrative department responsible for this job has been at work since the building was first put out to bid. This is a complicated and time-consuming task. First, the administrator must plan what specific equipment is needed for each of the various educational areas. Secondly, he must present his recommendations to the board of education and they, in turn, must give their approval to put these items out for bid.

Because boards of education normally do not meet more than once or twice a month, the process of getting these equipment bids out to vendors is a time-consuming task. And after the bids have been returned, they must be thoroughly examined to determine: (1) if the bidder has agreed to supply the exact item called for in the bids, and (2) which bidder has submitted the lowest price.

Then the board of education must accept the bid, and purchase orders must be made out listing all the items.

The first equipment which must be purchased is the type which is integrated into the building, such as hall lockers; science laboratory work areas which must be connected to the sewer, water, gas, and electric service; dust collectors for the wood shops; the dishwasher and stoves in the cafeteria kitchen, and the scores of like equipment which must be incorporated into the building before it is finished.

Most administrators, in planning equipment purchasing for a new high school, will make use of a set of blueprints, either pasting in replicas of the equipment cut to scale size, or marking the plans with colored pencil, writing in the name of the product. This assures the administrator that, when it comes time to move in to the building, there

25

will be no deficiency in needed equipment which could seriously affect the educational program.

Most school superintendents rely heavily on high school department heads and principals when they are compiling bids to furnish a new high school. If there is no existing high school staff from which the superintendent can draw the needed information, it will be necessary for him to hire the department heads and other needed personnel prior to the completion of the building, usually on a part-time basis.

All too often the cost of the building exceeds the budgeted amount set aside for its completion. This comes about through unexpected change orders. As a consequence, the money budgeted for equipment and supplies is often tapped to pay for the added building expenses.

For this reason it is important that interested parents and the public in general make a check to determine if the educational program in a new high school building is being shortchanged because money has been taken from the equipment account.

To do this the following check list and evaluation can be used effectively:

Place an x in the appropriate space below the number which best indicates the degree to which the school district has supplied the basic equipment. Items such as student desks, teachers' desks, filing cabinets, etc. have not been included, nor have such departments as English or social studies, which require no special equipment.

Department and Subject or area	*Basic Equipment*	1 2 3 4 5
Auditorium	Comfortable seating (architect will indicate number and position)	
	Sound System	
	Spotlights)	
	Footlights)	
	Electronic control panel	
	Curtains	
	Motion picture booth	
	Electric-powered roll down screen	
	Sets	
Gymnasium	Parallel bars, etc.	
	Mats	
	Ropes	
	Volley ball nets	
	Glass-backed basketball baskets	
	Ping Pong table and accessories	
	Balls, bats, mitts, protective masks, uniforms for all sports, football	

Department and Subject or area	Basic Equipment	1 2 3 4 5
	gear, etc.	
	Locker room benches	
	Team lockers	
	Class lockers	
Weight Lifting Room	At least five types of weight lifting equipment	
Athletic Fields	Baseball and softball cages, benches (or dugout), bases.	
	Outdoor baskets with black-topped area	
	Fenced-in tennis courts, nets	
	High jump hurdles	
	Football, baseball scoreboards	
	Equipment storage building	
	Pole vault equipment	
	Soccer, football goal posts	
	Golf clubs	
	White-lining machine	
Art: Painting and Drawing	Drawing boards	
	Easels	
	Moveable platform for posing	
	Storage units for supplies	
	Storage units for student work	
Crafts	Supply cabinets	
	Student work drawers or lockers	
Ceramics	Electric or gas kilns	
	Electric clay mixers	
	Sinks	
	Electric potter's wheels	
	Molding boards	
	Wet-clay depositories	
	Supply cabinets	
	Storage units for student work	
Science: Biology	At least 12 student lab stations, each containing water, electricity, gas, sink and two stools	
	Specimen tray, scalpels, etc.	
	Fish tank	
	Student desiccators	
	Lab carts	
	Animal and bird cages	
	At least 15 microscopes	
	Television receiver	

Department and Subject or area	*Basic Equipment*	1 2 3 4 5
	Movie screen	
	Chart stand and charts	
	Bunsen burners	
	Storage units	
	Specimens and containers for specimens	
Chemistry	At least 12 laboratory stations containing water, electricity, gas, sink, acid-proof tops and two stools	
	12 Bunsen burners	
	12 each petri dishes, test tubes, etc.	
	Centrifuge	
	Ring stands	
	Lab carts	
	Test tube racks	
	Chart stand and charts	
	Movie screen	
	Television	
	Cabinets with locks for storage of chemicals	
Physics	At least 12 lab stations containing water, electricity, gas, sink and two stools	
	Weights, pulleys, inclined planes, etc.	
	Balance beam, scales	
	Geiger counter	
	Stroboscope	
	Multi-meters	
	Barometer, hygrometer, thermometer	
	Laser	
	Spectroscope	
	Emergency eye wash station	
	Incubator	
	Microprojector	
	Lab carts	
	Gyroscope	
	Inertia apparatus	
	Force board	
	Newtonian demonstrator	
	Centripetal force apparatus	
	Osmosis apparatus	
	Open manometer	
	Boyle's law apparatus	

Department and Subject or area	*Basic Equipment*	1	2	3	4	5
	Hydrometer					
	Resonance apparatus					
	Calorimeter					
	Electrolysis apparatus					
	Tuning forks					
	Chart stand and charts					
	Telescopes					
	Spectroscope					
	Movie screen					
	Television					
	Storage units for supplies					
Foreign Language: Language Laboratory	Minimum 25-booth language laboratory with multi-master tape decks, student listen-student repeat capabilities, microphones and headsets, control panel at each booth. Teacher-listening capabilities and teacher correction capabilities					
Home Economics: Sewing	At least 15 electric sewing machines with cabinets					
	Layout tables					
	Dressing rooms with mirrors					
	Full length mirrors on stands					
	Platform for modeling					
	Washer and dryer					
	Irons, ironing boards					
	Storage cabinets for supplies					
	Storage units for students' work					
Cooking	At least 12 stoves, both electric and gas, if available					
	Pots, pans, utensils, silverware, blenders, etc.					
	Refrigerators					
	Cooling racks					
	Supply cabinets					
	Dish washers					
	Freezers					
	Microwaves					
Home Management, Child-Development Courses	Dining room table and chairs					
	Table settings (dishes, silverware, glasses, etc.)					
	Doll houses, dolls, toy trucks and					

Department and Subject or area	*Basic Equipment*	1 2 3 4 5
	autos, games, educational toys, children's stoves and cookware, balls, etc.	
	Piano	
	Record player, children's records	
	Television	
	Sleeping mats	
	Toy musical instruments	
Outdoor Area for Child Development Courses	Slides, merry-go-round, swings see-saw, jungle gym	
Industrial Arts: Wood	12 work benches, each containing two work stations	
	Two wood lathes	
	Two or three radial arm saws	
	Milling machine	
	Two table saws	
	Two band saws	
	Planer-shaper-jointer	
	Two drill presses	
	Two or three electric grinders	
	Dust removal system at each power tool	
	Electric hand tools: skill-saws, drills, planes, routers, jig saws, sanders (belt and finishing)	
	12 sets hand tools	
	Sectional framework of portion of house, including framing for window and door	
	Steel lumber storage rack	
	Storage cabinets for tools	
	Storage cabinet for students' work	
	Spray painting equipment	
	Wet-dry vacuum	
Metal Shop	12 work benches with two student work areas	
	Four or five metal lathes	
	Four or five brakes	
	12 sets hand tools	
	Electric drills, burnishers, grinding wheels, soldering guns, etc.	
	Forge and anvil	

Department and Subject or area	*Basic Equipment*	*1 2 3 4 5*
Electrical Shop	Acetylene torches Arc welders Storage cabinets for tools and supplies Storage cabinet for students' work 24 student work positions containing voltmeter, ohmmeter, ammeter and snap-on circuit board assembly 24 wiring kits for radio construction Framed house wall with electric wiring, receptacles, two-way switches, lighting, circuit breaker box Television model with schematic Chart stand and charts Cabinets for storage	
Graphic Arts	Two or three offset presses Folding machine One or two plate burning processors Vari-typer or equivalent Dark room with automatic developers and enlargers Letterpress Type, type cases and stands, chases, brass rule, quads, leads, composing sticks, etc. Electric paper cutter with safety lock Drying racks Storage cabinets for fluids, inks, paper and other supplies	
Vocational Education	Courses now offered in American high schools are too numerous to give detailed equipment lists. Most common courses: (check off a "5" for each course offered in your school system) auto mechanics auto collision repair small engine repair construction industries: electrical plumbing carpentry	

Department and Subject or area	Basic Equipment	1	2	3	4	5
	masonry					
	heating/air conditioning					
	agriculture					
	husbandry					
	forestry					
	food management					
	hotel/motel management					
	distributive education					
	radio and TV repair					
	clock repair					
	lawn/garden maintenance					
	R.O.T.C.					
	aircraft maintenance					
	retail sales					
	practical nursing					
	teachers' assistant					
Mechanical Drawing/Drafting	24 drafting tables with stools and T-squares					
	Two blueprint copiers					
	Rulers, triangles, french curves, etc.					
	Pantograph					
	Templates					
	24 drawing boards					
	Individual illumination at each table					
	Storage cabinets for supplies					
	Storage drawers for students' work					
Business Education	24 computers (several makes advisable)					
	24 printers (some dot matrix, some letter quality); printers are a component part of each computer					
	Large screen television					
	Pull-down movie screen					
	Film projector					
Typing	24–30 electric typewriters					
	24–30 typing desks					
	Metronome					
	Desk top book holders					
	Pull down chart rack and charts					

Department and Subject or area	Basic Equipment	1 2 3 4 5
	Tape player	
	Record player	
Stenography/ Bookkeeping/ Distributive Education/ Work Study	24–30 large, flat-topped student desks with drawers	
	Tape player	
	Chart stand	
	Electric adding machines	
	Mimeograph machine	
Merchandising	Simulated store display window unit	
	Electronic cash registers	
	Clothes manikins	
	Mimeograph machine	
	Small offset press	
	Typewriters	
	Merchandising display racks with a variety of display materials	
	Storage units	
	Television set	
Cafeteria/Kitchen	Sufficient folding tables and benches to seat one-third of the student body	
	Trays	
	Silverware and plates (or plasticware)	
	Dishwasher	
	Stoves/ovens	
	Walk in freezer with stainless steel shelving	
	Refrigerators	
	Large-volume electric mixers	
	Pots, pans, etc. (overhead hanging units)	
	At least two serving lines with tray supports, hot and cold dispensing units, milk coolers, ice cream dispensers, and cash registers	
	Garbage receptacles	
	Storage shelves in vermin-proof room	
Central Offices	Counter to separate outer office	
	Teachers' mailboxes	
	Files, desks, chairs	
	Telephone switchboard	
	Intercom system to classrooms	

Department and Subject or area	Basic Equipment	1	2	3	4	5
	Master clock					
	Mimeograph/offset machine					
	Electric typewriters					
	Collating machine					
	Folding machine					
	Postage meter					
	Storage cabinets					
	Master computer					
Health Suite	Cots					
	Medicine cabinet with lock					
	Scale					
	Audiometer					
	Dental chair					
	Examining table					
	Medical equipment (to be determined by school physician)					
	Stethoscope					
	Blood pressure equipment					
Music	30+ music stands and chairs					
	Piano					
	Band and orchestral instruments, depending upon policy of school board: student-owned/rented or supplied by school					
	Tiered platform for band or choral groups					
	Podium for music director					
	Storage room, cabinets or lockers for musical instruments; lockable					
Media Center	Book stacks					
	Card catalogs (or computer)					
	Footstools (if stacks are high)					
	Charging desk					
	Turnstile (or other type of exit control system)					
	Bulletin boards					
	Mimeograph					
	Tables, chairs					
	Record players (in booths)					
	All types of audio-visual equipment					
	Microfiche					
	Newspaper/magazine racks					
	Display cabinets					

Department and Subject or area	*Basic Equipment*	*1 2 3 4 5*
	Storage cabinets ·	
	Special table for "Readers' Guide to Periodical Literature" volumes	
Teachers' Room	Easy chairs, tables, couch, lamps, carpet, soda and food dispensers	
	Mimeograph machine	
	Duplicator	
	Water cooler	
All Department Offices	At least 3 movie projectors on carts	
	Two slide projectors	
	Camcorder and two VCR's	
	Two record players	
	Audio tape recorder	
	Three portable television sets	

The elementary school is a far less expensive building to equip. However, there are some areas which are similar to the high school. For instance, most elementary schools today will have specialized rooms that need specialized equipment if they are to function adequately, such as general science, health, and gymnasiums.

Science rooms should contain basic equipment for the teaching of general science, which consists of the fundamentals of biology, chemistry, physics, geology, ecology, astronomy, meteorology, and related subjects. Specific recommendations for materials and equipment which should be provided for an elementary general science room are given below in the evaluation.

In a smaller elementary school the health education room may be combined with the science room. Equipment for an elementary health classroom is also given below in the evaluation.

The elementary school gymnasium, used primarily by the upper grades, should contain most of the paraphernalia and equipment that is listed above under the high school requirements.

Boys and girls in grades four and higher participate in many of the same sports that their older high school brothers and sisters are participating in. However, the elementary pupil is at a stage where he is learning the fundamentals of these games and activities, and is becoming adept in them, and therefore some of the specialized equipment is not needed.

The following evaluation for the elementary school contains a list of equipment which should be found in the self-contained classroom, in the grade levels as noted.

Evaluation

Place an x below each entry; 1 if not furnished, 5 if furnished. Then connect the x's with a continuous line to form a graph.

1 2 3 4 5

- Preschool and Kindergarten:
    - Doll houses
    - Dolls
    - Doll carriages
    - Educational toys
    - Educational puzzles
    - Toy cars, fire trucks, etc.
    - Ambulatory toys (tricycles, wagons, etc.)
    - Crayons, crayoning books, etc.
    - Picture books
    - Sleeping mats or cots
    - Game equipment
    - Toy telephones
    - Toy stoves and other kitchen equipment and utensils
    - Phonographs, movie projector, screen, televisions, etc.
- Primary Grades
    - Extensive classroom library
    - Bulletin boards
    - Alphabet placards
    - Flash cards
    - Reading laboratory (or centrally located one, possibly in the media center)
    - Globe
    - Penmanship charts
- Middle and Upper Grades
    - Maps and charts
    - Globe
    - History charts
    - Flash cards
    - Bulletin boards, display cases
    - Models (Examples: "Construction of a western fort of the early 1800's" or "The Interior of a Hogan")
    - Classroom library
    - Television

1 2 3 4 5

- Special Rooms: General Science
  - Telescope
  - Microscopes
  - Weather station
  - Test tubes, etc.
  - Models (Volcanoes, etc.)
  - Charts
  - Pictures
  - Aquarium, cages
  - Specimens
  - Lift pump model
  - Molecule model
  - Electrolyte
  - Magnetic weather map
  - Fault model, folding mountain model
  - Sedimentation chamber
  - Magnets/electromagnets, motors, generator
  - Bell/light current board
  - Series/parallel circuits boards
  - Polarizer
  - Prisms, lenses
  - Greenhouse unit, hydroponics
  - Balance beam
  - Wheel and axle, acceleration pump
  - Pulleys
  - Planet model
  - Rocket model
- Health Classroom
  - Charts: nutrition, diseases and their symptoms, male and female sex organs, drug and alcohol abuse, anatomy, teeth, pregnancy, and birth
  - Skeleton
  - Replicas: eye, ear

Chapter Four

THE ELEMENTARY SCHOOL CURRICULUM

A school might be compared to a restaurant; the cooks and waiters are the teachers, the diners are the students, and the food which is served to the students by the teachers is the curriculum.

The curriculum of a school is contained in a series of courses of study. A course of study contains the following parts: General objectives, specific objectives, subject matter to be covered, texts to be used, and evaluations of student achievement.

Other information may also be included, such as audiovisual material available for teacher and student use, work sheets and workbooks for student use, sample tests, bibliographies, student projects which the teacher may assign, and review procedures.

In preparing these courses of study, it is important that there is input from many different sources. Often parents, students, teachers, administrators and community leaders are involved to some extent. But the ultimate task of conceiving each course of study, putting it into writing, and editing the finished product falls primarily on the teaching staff.

In a new school about to be opened, the faculty (or a representative portion of the faculty) is employed during the summer months prior to the opening of school.

Courses of study are written by the teachers of the grade level where they will be used. But it is also important that each grade level course of study be integrated with the one that follows it and with the one which precedes it. In fact, the entire body of knowledge which the school wishes to give to its pupils from the time they enter until they leave should first be developed before any work is begun on individual grade levels.

In schools which have been in operation for a while, these courses of study should be reviewed about every five years and changes made to reflect the developments in educational philosophy that have occurred and also changes in student body make-up.

It is unfortunate that in many school districts not all teachers follow the courses of study which have been prepared for their use. Recently, a principal of an elementary school, concerned about the lack of attention her teachers were paying to recently revised courses of study, made a visit to each classroom in the building, and on a pretext, asked each teacher to make a correction on one of the pages. Nearly 90 percent of the teachers either couldn't find their copy of the course of study or located it only after a great deal of searching.

When questioned, several of the "old-timer" teachers explained that they had taught the grade for so long they knew each step in every subject area like they knew their way to work.

On the other hand, one may visit school systems, particularly in the larger cities, where on a particular day every teacher in the school system is teaching the exact same topic in the exact same way, leaving no room for originality nor innovation. I would suggest that a happy marriage between the two extremes lends itself to the most successful kind of teaching.

The task of the elementary school is to teach the "basics." There is no argument as to what constitutes the "bedrock" of elementary education: Reading, 'riting and 'rithmetic, the three R's. Next in importance are such subjects as science (given a big boost when the USSR sent up its first sputnik), social studies, language arts (of which reading is a part), health, physical education, art, and music. Foreign languages are sometimes included for upper-grade elementary school pupils.

In addition, many state legislatures have mandated other subjects such as the dangers of drug and alcohol consumption, sex education, the dangers of talking to strangers, fire prevention and how to escape from one's home in the event of a fire. The list goes on and on, depending upon the particular "pet grieves" of certain legislators.

Because there are only so many minutes in a pupil's school day, every time the state mandates a subject which must be taught, it takes time away from the basic subjects.

The remainder of this chapter will discuss in detail the essentials of each course of study in grades one through eight for the subjects enumerated above.

Evaluation

Rate each entry 1–5 by placing an x beneath the number. (1 is low; 5 is high) Then connect all the x's with a continuous line to form a graph.

1 2 3 4 5

- Your child's school has prepared courses of study in all subject areas
- Your child's school revises its courses of study at least every five years
- Parents, civic leaders, administrators, and teachers were included in the preparation of the courses of study
- Courses of study are integrated within grades and between grades
- All teachers refer constantly to their courses of study and follow them
- The majority of school time is spent teaching the basics

LANGUAGE ARTS

Primary Grades. During these years reading and writing are the two subjects which are given the majority of class time. The two subjects are interrelated and are often taught together.

During the first three grades, pupils are divided into about three groups, depending upon the ability and how far advanced each child has progressed. Each group may be assigned different reading books and workbooks, or all may be reading from the same text, but at different levels.

More and more schools are returning to the use of flash cards, particularly when working with slower learners. Flash cards can be made interesting to the class by dividing the group into teams and keeping score. Relay races are fun, too; a student running up to a pile of flash cards, selecting one, giving the correct answer and returning to tag the next player on his team.

The modern elementary school has opted for a combination of "sight reading" and phonics. The two seem to be a happy marriage. Sight reading satisfies a pupil's needs during most of his reading time; phonics takes over when he meets a word with which he is not familiar and with which he has difficulty pronouncing.

Pupils who fall behind in reading ability during the primary grades, and who receive no remedial instruction to bring them up to grade level, are invariably dropouts in the ninth and tenth grades. The inability to read with at least a sixth-grade level of speed and comprehension is the primary cause of failure in *all* subjects in the upper elementary grades and in high school.

For this reason it is vital that every elementary school have remedial instruction *that starts during the first and second grades* and continues until every student has reached his potential.

Remedial reading instruction requires a specially trained teacher, usually one with a master's degree in remedial teaching. She or he should have a room equipped with the necessary testing equipment and with an adequate supply of reading material for all reading levels. Many remedial instructors like to work with reading laboratories because more students can be helped at a given time. Reading laboratories are programmed with units of work which, when completed satisfactorily, allow the pupil to continue on with the next lesson at his or her own rate of speed.

The remedial reading teacher, in the meantime, can be working with another student. If the child at the laboratory has difficulty, the teacher is close by to give assistance.

In first grade children begin to learn how to write. This learning process should be closely integrated with reading. Words learned during reading class should be incorporated into the written lesson.

In these early grades children write letters—to famous people, to their parents, to other relatives, to the editor of the local newspaper. They also write stories—from their imagination or about actual experiences they have gone through.

The teacher should be ready to help each child in the class by going about the room offering suggestions, spelling unfamiliar words, and by providing instruction on how to construct proper margins and paragraphs.

It is extremely important that children learn both printed and cursive letters at the same time, and that the teacher stress cursive writing over printing. This author has worked with a number of intelligent, scholarly, high school students who did all their written work by printing. When questioned, they admitted that somewhere along in the middle grades, they had not switched to cursive writing, and all their teachers had accepted their work and had never commented about the printing nor attempted to change their habit.

"Do you know how to write cursively?" I asked.

"Yes. But nobody can read it. And I can write faster this way," was the usual answer.

Experiments have proven otherwise; cursive writing is by far the faster method.

These students will have great difficulty in college.

As a student advances through the grades, the use of cursive writing becomes more and more important when speed becomes increasingly essential.

Simple grammar is introduced in the primary grades. Children at this age should become aware of the make-up of sentences and paragraphs, the use of some of the more frequent punctuation marks, and capitalization.

Middle Grades. During the middle grade years, a child's reading skills are being used in all his subject areas. This is a time when he is expanding his reading vocabulary, increasing his reading speed and growing in his ability to comprehend and assimilate what he is reading.

Reading teachers at these grade levels should be working with students to give them techniques which increase speed and comprehension. Skimming should be taught and each student should become proficient in this skill whenever he must search through voluminous material for isolated facts or figures.

He should learn how to quickly pick out the topic sentence of each paragraph, usually the first or the last. He should be aware that the remainder of the paragraph fills in the detail and completes the topic sentence.

Scanning is another technique that should be introduced during the middle grades. The ability to scan will be of great help to students as they advance through the upper grades, when studying for tests, when doing research, and when reading new material.

Part of the reading program during the middle grades concentrates on learning to follow written directions. The teacher should provide actual life-situations, if possible, directions the students will be required to use in later life: filling out job applications, completing questionnaires, following instructions for putting together a bicycle or some toy, learning the rules of a new game. Life is filled with instructions, and many adults have never learned how to cope adequately with them.

Reading in the middle grades is less formalized than in the primary grades. More reading is done by the students on their own or as part of an assignment. Book reports are usually required beginning about the third or fourth grade.

Class reading is often conducted by the entire class reading a book aloud, each student taking a turn. The teacher is able to help any student who indicates that he is having difficulty with certain words. If the reading inadequacy is pronounced, the teacher should arrange to have the student visit the remedial reading teacher who can then analyze the problem and prescribe therapeutic measures to correct the deficiencies.

Written expression at this age level becomes more sophisticated. All subject areas beside language arts require written work in the form of answers to teacher-assigned questions, or questions taken from the textbook. Essays and term papers are often assigned, too.

Two new areas of the language arts subject are introduced during the middle grades: spelling and vocabulary-building. Often the two are combined. Usually new words are introduced to the class on Monday; the teacher goes over the words with the class, pronouncing them, conducting a student-oriented practice spelling session, and then assigning homework which will give the class practice in learning to spell the words and in using them in sentences.

On Friday the class will be given a test to determine how well it has mastered the spelling and meaning of the words.

Another part of the language arts curriculum in the middle grades is assisting pupils to become proficient speakers and listeners. Periodically the teacher will make an assignment for each student to be prepared to talk to the class about a hobby, an exciting event in the student's life or to give directions on how to reach a particular location in town or how to make or repair some object.

Often at the end of each student's presentation, the rest of the class will be called upon to make helpful suggestions for improving the talk, or they may be required to keep a scorecard for each presentation for such qualities as posture, clarity, enunciation, and interest.

Formal grammar is an important part of the language arts program during these years. Parts of speech and their use in a sentence are emphasized. Workbooks or ditto sheets are used extensively to fortify the instruction. Understanding simple, compound, complex, run-on, and incomplete sentences are a part of the language arts program.

All too often, however, the teaching of grammar is isolated from the student's needs as a writer of the English language. *Functional Grammar* is a term which has come into vogue, and its connotation implies that grammar as an isolated subject is useless. Unless the student incorporates what he has learned into his writing skills, even an extensive understanding of grammatical use is wasted.

For this reason one of the best ways to teach grammar is through a thorough examination by the teacher of all written work turned in by a student. Comments in the margins by the teacher will call attention to the errors that have been made. A follow-through by the teacher in the form of a brief but thorough oral explanation of the correct form is a must. Furthermore, the student should be required to rewrite and resubmit the paper making all corrections.

In many elementary schools today in which the upper classes are departmentalized, the language arts teacher is given an extra "preparation period" to compensate for the many hours of work required to correct student compositions.

Upper Grades. Rarely is reading taught as a separate subject in the upper grades. By this time all students should be reading at or above grade level. Various reading tests, administered each year, assist the teachers, guidance department, and the administration to ascertain the reading level of each student. Those who have fallen behind during the middle grades have been afforded remedial instruction, and hypothetically all have now reached their normal reading level.

Unfortunately, this is not always the case, and further remedial work may be necessary even at the upper elementary grade levels. There is a certain stigma attached to receiving this kind of help in the eyes of upper grade students, and many of them will resist further remedial help. In the inner cities in particular, this is a problem faced by school authorities.

Too many teen-agers are facing life without the reading skills needed in modern-day society. The problem is augmented by the alarming dropout rate occurring in the upper elementary and lower high school grades. The very students who need remedial help the most are the ones who are dropping out of school as soon as they may legally do so. And those who are forced to remain in school because they are under age, rebel against the authority of the school and refuse the remedial help they so desperately need.

The dropout problem is caused by many factors: lack of interest and boredom, the lure of the streets and gang membership, easy money, drug addiction, alcohol abuse, teenage parenthood, poor grades, teachers who "turn them off," and arrest and conviction of a crime.

Reading in the upper grades of the elementary school is taught in "literature" classes. The classics given to us by past masters, and modern-day best sellers provide the reading material. Usually the students do the reading as a homework assignment. The following day the teacher will discuss what has been read with the class, clarifying any portion that has caused difficulty, discussing with the students the main characters in the book, pointing out the novel's theme, and relating the lives of these characters to the lives of the students.

Book reports will also be assigned. The number of reports required will run from a minimum of two to as many as a dozen for the school year. Extra credit may be given for exceeding the required number, an incentive which attracts the advanced reader and fails to interest the slow reader.

Book reports, as a means of accentuating the amount of reading done by the poorer readers, has not proven effective. A student in an eighth-grade class who was reading on a fourth grade level once told me, "I read the first chapter and the last chapter, and that's all I need to do to fool the teacher into thinking I read the whole book."

Another student once confided to me, "I choose a book that's been made into one of those classic funny books. Then I read the funny book and make my report from that. It takes me maybe a half an hour."

Or, "I pick a book that's been made into a movie, one I can rent at the video shop. The teacher says no, we can't do that, but she doesn't know much about what films are on tape. All she does is check the papers to see what's playing in the movie houses. I get away with it all the time."

When teachers are challenged by such evidence, their usual response is, "A little reading by a slow reader is better than none at all." And there's a germ of truth in what they say. The students quoted above probably would turn in no book report at all if they weren't able to find an easy solution to their reading problem.

In fact, some homogeneous classes built around slow learners use funny books and books published specially for below grade readers. These books contain characters and episodes which appeal to early teenagers, but are written in simple style and contain no difficult words.

Grammar at this stage in the student's school career consists of a review of what has been taught in the lower grades—parts of speech, sentence structure, punctuation, and capitalization—and new material such as agreement of a subject with its predicate, agreement of a pronoun with its antecedent, conjugation of irregular verbs, and nominative, objective, and possessive cases of pronouns.

Exercises in speaking and listening are less formal than in the lower grades. Class discussions, teacher demonstrations, and an occasional student report satisfy these requirements.

Note taking is stressed, particularly in classes homogeneously grouped with college-bound students. Some schools teach an abbreviated form of shorthand, and students are required to use it so they can become proficient in taking down the important points of a lecture or class discussion.

Other schools may permit and even encourage the use of audio tape recorders for the college bound. The students are then required to make notes from their tapes at home and submit them to the teacher for evaluation. Tape recorders are an accepted method of note taking among college students.

Spelling and vocabulary building is continued throughout the upper elementary grades and into high school. Teachers should encourage students to make the words in their vocabulary lists become a part of their writing experience. Learning the spelling and meaning of words in isolation is a meaningless and time-wasted experience.

Evaluation

Rate each of the following by placing an x below the number best describing the conditions in your community's elementary school. If you are rating more than one school, indicate x's for each school. Then connect the x's for each school separately to form individual graphs. You may wish to use different colored pencils to distinguish between schools. Comparisons can be made between schools.

1 2 3 4 5

- Reading and writing are stressed in the primary grades and are integrated.
- Both "sight reading" and phonics are taught in the primary grades.
- The school has a remedial reading teacher and a well-equipped reading laboratory.
- The teachers in the primary grades are always about the room helping children, or are working with a reading group.
- Both printed and cursive writing is taught at the same time.
- In the middle grades, speed and comprehension are stressed.
- Scanning and skimming are two techniques taught in the middle grades.
- All students have an opportunity to read aloud to the class.
- Teachers assign written compositions at least once a week. Papers are corrected in detail.
- Spelling and vocabulary are taught on a regular basis in the middle and upper grades.
- Literature is taught in the upper grades.
- Functional grammar is taught in the middle and upper grades. All papers turned in by students are thoroughly checked for grammatical errors and students are required to rewrite their papers, making corrections.
- Book reports are required.
- Homogeneous grouping for reading is scheduled.
- Note-taking is stressed.

MATHEMATICS

Primary Grades. There has been much controversy in the past few years concerning the success of the "new math" and whether it might now be time to revert back to the old way of teaching arithmetic. The "new math" simply put, uses the algebraic approach to solving problems. Therefore all calculations are put in equation form.

In the lower grades, therefore, instead of solving the addition problem

$$\begin{array}{r} 1 \\ + 1 \\ \hline 2 \end{array}$$

it is expressed as $1 + 1 = 2$.

In the lower grades the differences between the two systems are negligible, but as the student advances through the grades, the gap widens.

For a student who will go on to algebra and other forms of higher mathematics the "new math" is the preferable system because the student has been taught from the beginning to think a problem through as an equation.

Teaching the basics of addition, subtraction, multiplication, and division has returned, to some extent, to rote memory. Flash cards are returning to the classroom. There are those who argue that memorization of these table is no longer necessary with the invention of the calculator and the computer, but it should be remembered that there are many times when no calculator is at hand and one must resort to the old fashioned method of using one's "mental calculator."

It is important during these early years of a pupil's education that a teacher make arithmetic meaningful. Too often arithmetic is taught abstractly, as may be the case if flash cards are the sole method of instruction.

The best method is to teach the mechanics first and then apply this knowledge to actual life situations, life situations that are meaningful to the child. Example: A teacher of first grade has used flash cards to the point where the class has memorized some of the more basic additions. It is now appropriate to transfer this knowledge to life-situations.

"Two children stand up—you, Shirley, and you, Peter. There, we have two children who are going to play a game. But Sally comes by and so does Elizabeth. Two more children are ready to play. How many children are there? Yes, four. Two and two are four."

There are many ways an innovative teacher can make arithmetic come alive. Besides her own imagination, she has at her side many published workbooks which are so designed that the student can visualize the meaning of numbers and how they influence people's lives. These workbooks are designed to capture a child's attention; many of the pages are filled with mathematical games and puzzles, and pictures to be colored.

Much akin to the workbooks described above, is the ditto master. Many primary teachers make use of these commercially-prepared masters. From them a teacher can reproduce sufficient copies for her entire class, and the master can be put away to be used another year. These masters contain much the same type of material as a workbook, and the expense is considerably less.

Mathematics, like remedial reading, makes use of the laboratory approach to learning. A mathematics laboratory can be as simple as a few well-chosen materials placed on a table away from the rest of the class where children can go when they have completed their assigned seat work.

On the other extreme, a mathematics laboratory can be housed in a separate room where individual booths, separated from one another, will allow each child complete quiet. Here the child will have access to a computer which will be programmed to provide a sequence of lessons, each of which must be mastered before the computer will allow the pupil to go on to the next lesson.

If he has trouble at one stage, the computer has auxiliary lessons on the same level. Once these auxiliary lessons have been completed satisfactorily, the pupil is then urged to continue to the next level. And some computer programs will praise the child for how well he has done!

In addition to the computer programs, each booth may have access to filmstrips, films, audio and video tapes, and supplementary books.

The mathematics laboratory permits a student to advance at his own rate of speed. It also teaches him to work independently, often without supervision. A mathematics laboratory is well worth the cost.

Middle Grades. In the primary grades, addition and subtraction are covered, as well as simple problem-solving. In the middle grades, the teacher first reviews what the class has learned in first and second grades (and probably forgotten over the summer). Once the review has been completed, the class is then ready to begin work on multiplication, and finally, toward the end of the year, on division.

The use of flash cards, workbooks, ditto sheets, and the mathematics laboratory are all tools which the teacher of a middle grade uses. Problem-solving is just as important here as it was in the lower grades.

Upper Grades. After a review of multiplication and division, the upper grade teacher is ready to introduce fractions, decimals, and percentages. Fractions, in particular, require a great deal of time to get across to many students. They have great difficulty in learning how to multiply, add, subtract, and divide them.

Because of the wide differences in learning ability, many schools separate students into homogeneous groups during the seventh and eighth grade. The lower groups take two years to complete fractions, decimals, and percentages. The upper groups probably will have time to begin the fundamentals of algebra and geometry, or to study such related topics as money management, the stock market, completing income tax forms, or simple bookkeeping.

Other schools solve the problem of individual differences by departmentalizing the seventh and eighth grade. In a large enough school departmentalization will permit several sections to be formed. Each section can be homogeneously grouped and the lower groups can be assigned to a teacher who has been trained to deal with remedial problems.

Evaluation

Rate each of the following statements by placing an x beneath the appropriate number. Then connect each x with a continuous line to form a graph.

1 2 3 4 5

- The "new math" is taught in my child's school. .
- Flash cards and other forms of rote memorization are used.
- Problem-solving is a part of the mathematics program.
- Workbooks and ditto master sheets are used.
- A well-equipped mathematics laboratory with a full-time remedial mathematics teacher is in operation.
- There is an orderly progression through the grades for the teaching of the basics, including addition, subtraction, multiplication, division, fractions, percentages, and decimals.
- Provision is made for the fast learner to begin elementary algebra in the upper grades.

SCIENCE

Primary Grades. Science in the lower elementary grades is centered about the child's place in the world. He is introduced to hundreds of other living beings that share his world in the form of animals and plants. Books with colored pictures of domestic and wild animals must be included in any class library. Insects, reptiles, fish, and other forms of life will interest this age group. Not only does the child want to see pictures of how they look, but he is interested in how they live and in stories about them.

Visits to the local zoo, if possible, should be included in the curriculum. If a zoo is not within travel distance, perhaps there is a farm in the area that can be the object of a field trip. Many cities have "petting farms" where children are permitted to become better acquainted with certain domesticated animals.

Children will bring their pets to school, and this practice should be encouraged. Facilities should be available to hold other animals such as hamsters, rabbits, snakes, mice, and baby chickens which may be a part of a rotating exhibit moved among classes in the lower grades.

Other aspects of the child's environment are also included in the primary science curriculum. Light, color, heat, sound, magnets can be the basis for interesting science experiments.

In recent years the emphasis of science in all grades has moved away from the acquisition of facts to an understanding of the "why" and "how" and to develop in the pupil a scientific approach to science. This is not to say that facts are not important; the "how" and the "why" are built upon a thorough understand of the basic facts.

"Hands on" science instruction must begin at an early age. Many of the experiments, no matter how simple in nature, must be done by the students themselves, not by the teacher in front of the class, although she may perform the experiment at the same time in order to show her pupils how it is to be done.

"Hands on" experiments require that equipment and supplies be made available by the board of education and not supplied by the teacher with her own funds, although this does not prevent her from gathering such material from nature or from free donations supplied by local merchants.

Middle Grades. This is the age group which is avidly interested in science and its related subjects. Boys and girls in the fourth, fifth, and sixth grades will attack a science project with fervor and excitement. In these classes such projects as model volcanoes, model airplanes and boats, electrical buzzers, human anatomy charts, telegraph keys, door bells, crystal radios, terrariums, and insect collections should be made available by the board of education.

In many schools the middle and upper grades share a common science room. In such an atmosphere a great many more experiments can be carried on than in the regular classroom. A general science room will contain pupil work stations where water, and sometimes gas and electricity are available. Secure storage areas are available to stow student work and protect it from other students or accidental breakage. Students are more likely to produce more advanced projects which require time and patience when they know their work will not be broken or lost.

The curriculum of the middle grades covers a wide range of the scientific field—the solar system, weather and climate, oceanography, ecology, electricity, the atmosphere, pollution, space, and basic geology.

Upper Grades. One of the aims of the upper grades' curriculum is to provide a basic foundation for students who will be taking the science courses in high school which lead to a college career, and to provide a pragmatic curriculum for the noncollege bound student. For this reason, as with the mathematics curriculum, some form of homogeneous grouping is essential to take care of individual differences. Departmentalization seems to work out best because the students can be scheduled so that the teachers to whom they are assigned are best qualified to work at their level.

The college-bound student is given basic knowledge in chemistry, biology, and physics. But more important, he is taught how to conduct an experiment, what equipment and supplies are available to him and how to use them, and how to avoid accidents and bodily harm.

In addition he is taught to think like a scientist, to know when the results of an experiment have proved the hypothesis he started out to prove.

During the seventh and eighth grades many boys and girls, through the science survey course described above, are able to determine which branch of science they wish to embark upon when they reach high school. Having made this decision, they can now concentrate on the courses which will best qualify them for entrance into the college of their choice.

For the student who does not plan to attend college, and for the student who does not have the ability to qualify for the college prep science course in seventh and eighth grade, a general science course is in order. This course should be an individualized program.

Peter, Sam, and Mary have decided to work as a team during those class periods when they are assigned to the science laboratory. Today, they are working on an experiment to prove that hot air is lighter than cold air and therefore rises.

Because they are working as a separate group from the rest of the class, they can proceed at their own rate. Before them on the lab table is a manual which gives them a step-by-step explanation of how to success-fully conclude their experiment. Also contained in the manual is a description of the desired outcome of each of the experiments, and a list of possible errors which the students might make and how they can determine if they have made any of them.

When Peter, Sam, and Mary have concluded this experiment, they will first write down the results in their notebooks. Following this they will include ways in which the scientific principle proven in the experi-ment is manifested in the world and in society. They will then take a self-test as a group, and if they are successful, will go on to the next experiment.

The test questions ask for few facts; instead they are oriented toward understanding the concepts of the experiment, toward appreciation of scientific values, and toward viable applications of the results in the everyday life of the student.

If at any time while they are working on an experiment, they run into trouble, they have several sources to which they can turn for assistance. Their textbook will be the first resource; the experiments in the manual are closely related to the material in the text. Also available are film-strips or video tapes showing how the experiment should be conducted. (These video tapes are taken of actual students in previous classes doing the experiment.)

Not all students in the class are working as a group. Some prefer to work alone, and this is an option that is open to them.

For extra credit students may turn in diagrams and charts which they have copied from those on file in the science lab or classroom. Or they may devise and construct projects at home which are not part of the assigned work.

Evaluation

Rate each of the following statements by placing an x beneath the appropriate score. Then connect the x's with a continuous line to form a graph.

1 2 3 4 5

• The science program for the primary grades centers about the child's immediate surroundings.
• Field trips are a part of the primary grade curriculum.

- Children are encouraged to bring their pets to school in the primary grades.
- Ample supplies are provided for the primary teachers by the board of education.
- Some form of individual instruction is provided in the middle and upper grades for students to proceed at their own rate.
- Student projects are encouraged in the middle and upper grades.
- Test questions ask for conclusions and understanding rather than facts.

SOCIAL STUDIES

In many schools social studies is one of the subjects which is not receiving the time and attention it should be given.

Part of the reason lies with the teacher. Many teacher-preparation colleges are not training elementary school teachers adequately in the social sciences.

Geography is the stepchild of the social studies curriculum. In my experience as an administrator, I have found that elementary school teachers are deficient in geographic knowledge. This is probably to be expected because the American population as a whole is not knowledgeable in this subject.

I recently overheard a conversation at an airport. Two companions were apparently about to depart for Tahiti, and they were arguing as to whether they would be flying into the setting sun or away from it.

"Tahiti is off the coast of Africa," one of the men said, "so naturally we'll be flying *east* and into the sun."

"Wrong!" exclaimed the other. "Tahiti is down off the coast of South America so we'll be flying *west.*"

And the two were leaving from the Newark airport!

Primary Grades. In the primary grades the curriculum is geared to introduce these six- and seven-year-old children to the immediate world in which they live. Discussions and lessons are centered about the child himself, his place in society, and what society has to offer him as he advances through life. Immediately following this, the topic shifts to the family and the child's place in it—what he owes the family and what the family should do for him.

Next the scene shifts to the child's community. He learns more about the police who are there to protect him. He hears about the life and duties of a fireman, a postman, the town fathers and how they make the laws that he must obey, and other municipal employees such as the garbage collectors and the street department workers.

This is the time when classes take many field trips to visit the people they are learning about and to see them in action. Many times representatives of these groups will come to the school and put on demonstrations and answer questions the children may pose.

Middle Grades. In the middle grades the sphere of interest broadens. Children of this age are interested in foreign peoples and how they live. The Indians of North and South America are studied. The Eskimos, the Incas, and the Mayas are all cultures which fascinate youngsters of this age group.

Student-made projects, maps, pictures, models, and essays are encouraged. Films are shown, television programs taped and replayed to the class. Groups of students write and put on skits and short plays.

Social studies, to be made vital and interesting to children of this age, must be graphic in design.

Another part of the curriculum of the middle grades is a study of past cultures. Among the topics covered: Columbus' journeys to the New World, further exploration and colonization by the English, Spanish, French, and Dutch; Medieval history with its glamorous tales of chivalry and the Crusades; Egyptian, Greek, and Roman history; and perhaps some mention of Oriental history.

Geography, unfortunately, usually is tied to history and is mentioned only incidentally as the occasion requires it. Modern educators could do well to look back to the early part of this century when geography was an important elementary subject and students learned about the hemispheres, the continents, and oceans, and spent many happy hours constructing maps, often from memory, of the places they had studied.

The legislature of the State of New Jersey is considering a bill sponsored by Joseph A. Palaia that would require all New Jersey public schools to provide education in world geography. "All studies have shown an abysmal ignorance of world geography among today's students," said Palaia. "Not too long ago some New Jersey students, when asked to locate Brazil on the map, began their search halfway around the world in Asia. "If you can't find a country on a map, identify its major cities, or name its primary products, I don't see how you can function in the global marketplace," concluded the assemblyman.

Upper Grades. In seventh grade there is usually an in-depth review of ancient civilizations. In addition, current events is introduced and students are encouraged to read the newspapers. Many schools purchase sufficient copies of a local paper that covers the national and international scene. Many social studies teachers in these grades will devote ten or fifteen minutes at the beginning of each class to go over the events of the day before and discuss their significance.

In eighth grade the usual subject in most schools is United States History and "civics." The first half of the school year covers history from the landing of the Pilgrims to the Civil War, and during the second semester, from the Civil War to the present. And before these students graduate from high school they will be subjected to at least two more years of American history, in the eleventh and twelfth grades.

Here again, geography is a forgotten subject and, unfortunately, there will be no more opportunities for them to broaden their knowledge in this field before they graduate.

In many of the social studies classes that I have visited during my years as an administrator, I found that most of the teaching was fact-oriented. Teachers were interested in their students learning dates, events, and the names of important people. I believe that this type of instruction was perpetuated over the years by instructors who were content with the least demanding type of instruction. Work sheets and tests are far simpler to correct and grade when a single word or a phrase is all that is required for an answer.

To me this is not teaching history; what is required is an *understanding, appreciation, and concern for the lives of the people who lived during the period, and the problems they faced, and the solutions they found to correct them.*

Some facts, names and dates are needed in order to keep everything in true prospective, but they are incidental to an understanding and appreciation of the world that existed for eons before these children entered it. Good teaching of the social studies emphasizes the "why", not the "when" and the "who."

Here again as in the lower grades, films, charts, models, video tapes and field trips play an important part in the learning process.

Evaluation

Rate each statement below by placing an x underneath the number which best describes the conditions in your community's school. If there is more than one elementary school, each school may be rated individually. Then connect the x's with single lines to make a graph for each school. Different colored pencils may be used to differentiate between schools.

1   2   3   4   5

- Social studies is taught in all grades.
- Geography is a separate subject and is taught at least once each week.
- The primary social studies curriculum is centered around the child's immediate world.
- Frequent field trips about town are scheduled for the primary classes.
- In the middle grades topics such as these are covered: peoples of foreign lands, ancient civilizations, settlement of the New World, medieval history.
- Social studies becomes alive through the use of films, video tapes, field trips, student projects, maps, charts, and pictures.
- Facts play a secondary role in all teaching and testing

HEALTH AND SEX EDUCATION

Sex education is included with health because in many schools it is taught by the same teacher, and is usually a subtopic of the health curriculum.

Probably no other subject is more in the public limelight and more controversial than the teaching of sex in the elementary school. It took years for the public high schools to calm the public furor after the subject was introduced there. Now the scene has shifted to the elementary schools and the arguments of the antagonists are stronger and more compelling than they were when they attacked the high school.

Sex education in the high school, it is argued, is justified because this is the age when teenagers are maturing and when they are experimenting with sex for the first time. But statistics show that seventh and eighth graders are equally as active, and that sex education should be given *before* problems arise and these youngsters find themselves in trouble.

These arguments make good sense. And proponents of these arguments carry it one step further: sex education should not be something that is suddenly thrust upon children in fourth, fifth or sixth grades, like a bolt of lightning out of the blue. It should be introduced at an early age and should carry through a child's schooling until he or she graduates from high school.

Sex Education in the Primary Grades. Those schools that have included sex education from grades one through twelve, usually start in first grade with an explanation of the sanctity of marriage. In some schools the curriculum for either first or second grades includes a fairly graphic explanation of how a baby is born. By the end of the primary grades, a simple description of conception is forthcoming.

Sex Education in the Middle Grades and Upper Grades. Courses of study vary widely from school to school for the middle grades. In some schools dating, petting, and teenage intercourse are discussed, as well as a basic explanation of venereal diseases, including AIDS. In other schools, these topics are reserved for the upper grades and a more detailed picture of child birth and conception is given instead.

By the time a student enters high school he has been given a detailed account of the sexual process from conception to birth. He also has been exposed to pictures and diagrams of the human reproductory system, male and female. He has probably seen movies or videotapes of actual sperm making their way to the egg and the act of fertilization when one of the sperm reaches its target.

If the mores of the community permit, all students, male and female, have been given a thorough background in contraceptive measures to prevent pregnancy and venereal diseases.

The tendency in most schools is to mix boys and girls in the same class. Most administrators believe that the boys should know about menstruation and other female sex information, and in turn, the girls should be aware of the male point of view toward sex. Mixed classes, it is believed, tends to promote happier and more successful marriages later in the students' lives.

Not too many schools discuss homosexuality or sex abnormalities. If these topics are discussed at all, they are left to the high school.

Health Education in the Primary Grades. For these grades health education is limited in scope and depth. The following are examples of some of the topics included in a primary course of study: (1) a discussion of what foods are best and how they promote growth and good health (2) rules for cleanliness and good personal hygiene, (3) how to take care of the teeth, (4) the benefits of sufficient sleep, (5) dangers to avoid in the home (poisons, electrical shocks, drownings in swimming pools, dangerous tools, etc.).

Health Education in the Middle and Upper Grades. In the middle and upper grades the traditional topics for health education are apt to take a back seat in many schools. This is because modern-day society, and in many cases the legislatures of the states, have mandated other more timely topics.

At the top of the list is drug addiction and its effects on the human body. Closely allied, cigarette smoking, and not far behind comes alcohol abuse—all very timely topics with teenagers these days, because studies have shown that in some schools as many as 75 percent of the high school students have admitted to using one or more of these narcotics. Of the seventy-five percent, almost half said that they began smoking cigarettes as early as third grade, began drinking alcoholic beverages around sixth and seventh grade, tried "grass" at about the same time, and got involved with stronger drugs in seventh or eighth grades.

It must be pointed out, however, that these percentages are not representative of all school districts. A lot depends on the community, how vigilant the police force and the school administration have been in detecting and dealing with the problem before it becomes deep-rooted.

Unfortunately some school administrators close their eyes to the problem, or deny its existence, or make halfhearted attempts to solve it. Other schools started early when the alcohol and drug problem first manifest itself.

One school in Florida recently brought in dogs that had been trained to detect marijuana and crack and used them to sniff out any supplies hidden in students' lockers. Other school systems have used undercover agents from the police department to find out who has been supplying the student body.

In addition to teaching about tobacco, alcohol and narcotics, other health topics may be included in the curriculum: (1) anatomy of the human body including the circulatory system, muscles, organs, skeleton, glands, and nervous system; (2) genetics; (3) the diseases of the human race and how they can be prevented and cured; (4) first aid training.

Evaluation

Rate each of the following statements by placing an x beneath the appropriate number. Then connect the x's with a continuous line to form a graph.

1 2 3 4 5

- Sex education is taught from grade one through eighth grade.
- Dating, petting, teenage intercourse, venereal diseases, child birth, conception, the male and female sex organs, venereal diseases, and contraception are taught at some time during the elementary school years.

- A health education program exists from grades one through grade eight.
- The following topics are taught at some time in the child's elementary schooling: nutrition, personal hygiene, dangers to be aware of, drug abuse, alcohol abuse, tobacco addiction, anatomy, genetics, diseases, first aid training.

PHYSICAL EDUCATION

Primary Grades. Most school systems do not schedule formal classes in physical education for children in the primary years. During these early school years, "recess" is the accepted way of scheduling physical education. It is usually conducted by the classroom teacher, and is quite informal in nature.

The teacher may organize a game of dodgeball for those children who wish to play, or she may permit the children to organize their own games such as tag or hide-and-seek if they so choose, or the children may simply play on the slides, swings, seesaws and merry-go-round, or chase one another around the play yard as children of this age so love to do.

Recess for these grades usually does not last longer than twenty minutes or half an hour. At this age no uniforms are required, and during cold weather, children dress in their coats and mittens. Seldom are these classes scheduled to use the gymnasium during inclement weather unless, for some reason, the facility is not being used at that time by the children in the upper grades.

Physical Education in the Middle and Upper Grades. Beginning about third or fourth grade, a program of formal physical education training begins which will carry through until the child graduates from high school. Most states require a certain number of minutes of "gym" each week.

Pupils are introduced to a program which requires a change of clothes and a shower before returning to their regular class. It has been my observation, however, that very few schools enforce the "shower" rule, and as a result children get dressed in their street clothes, often while they are still wet with perspiration, which, unfortunately, defeats the purpose of changing into gym clothes.

Most physical education teachers will tell you that physical exercise is not the only purpose for having gym classes. They will tell you that they are instilling the qualities of self-discipline, fellowship, leadership, cooperation, sportsmanship, and self-confidence in the youngsters in their classes. But my observation of many classes in a number of schools has seen little evidence that such training is actually taking place.

Most physical education classes appear to have only two main goals: (1) Teach the children the rudiments of as many games as possible, and (2) Give them a good workout to improve their stamina and build up their muscles. This is not to say that both of these objectives are not commendable in themselves. We are living in an era when bodybuilding has become an important past time among the adult population, and the younger we start this type of training, the more likely that it will continue through a lifetime.

All physical education classes should start with some form of warm-up exercises, either calisthenics or running about the gymnasium for a few laps. During good weather, the activities for the entire period should be held outside.

The physical education instructor should monitor the dressing area both before and after class to insure the safety of the students.

The following is a list of activities and games which are acceptable for middle- and upper-grade physical education classes: track events, trampoline, tumbling, wrestling, touch football, yoga, ping-pong, kick ball, racquetball, shuffle ball, skating, speed ball, folk dancing, ballroom dancing, handball, gymnastics, field hockey, baseball, softball, archery, soccer, volleyball, tennis, golf, dodge ball, rhythms, aerobics, and corrective exercises.

Most schools in this country now arrange their classes so that boys and girls are scheduled together.

Evaluation

Rate each of the following statements by placing an x under the appropriate number. Then connect the x's with a continuous line to form a graph.

1 2 3 4 5

- All pupils during "recess" are engaged in some form of worthwhile activity.
- Students change into gym clothes in the middle and upper grades.
- All students take showers before dressing in their street clothes at the end of P.E. classes.
- Gym classes start with some form of warm-up exercise.
- The P.E. teachers monitor the locker room while students are there.

- Throughout the school year a wide variety of games are played.
- Boys and girls take gym classes together.

ART

The purpose of art education in the elementary school is definitely not to develop successful artists, but to give each boy and girl an opportunity to express himself or herself through the media of color, shape, harmony, light and shadow, and movement. The skilled art teacher never criticizes a child's work as long as the child has shown sincerity and purpose while composing his work.

Too frequently I have observed art classes where the teacher makes the decisions as to what form of art expression the class will practice on a particular day. "Now class, today we will all draw this vase I have placed here on the podium, and next period we will color it."

Perhaps Johnny doesn't really feel like drawing a vase that day. Perhaps he prefers to draw animals, or sketch airplanes in a dogfight, or perhaps he would be happier watching Sally in the next seat draw costume designs which she's so good at.

In all forms of the arts, inspiration is the keyword to producing results which satisfy the individual who produces it. A teacher has no right to impose her will on twenty-five or thirty children, all of whom are supposed to draw the same thing at the same time. In an adult art class, such authority would soon leave the teacher without any pupils; children have the same basic needs and they should receive the same consideration.

Primary teachers are less apt to make this mistake. They pass out crayons and sheets of drawing paper, and they don't even have to say to their class, "Now we're going to draw," because the children instinctively pick up the crayons and start to color. And do they all draw the same thing?

Children in the primary grades have no inhibitions when it comes to artwork. They draw what inspires them at the moment. Often adults have difficulty recognizing what some of the objects in these drawing represent, but this is immaterial. Each child must feel gratification and satisfaction when the drawing is finished, and he will have this if the teacher holds up all the drawings to show the others in the class and says nice things about each of them.

In the upper grades, diversification is the rule. The older child likes to experiment with many mediums. He is at the age of exploration, not just in art but in all his subjects.

He will try water colors one day, oils the next, clay on another occasion. He will whittle, weave, work with plaster and paper-maché, silkscreen, and raffia. It is a period in a young person's life when he is testing himself and opening up many doors until he finds the one that satisfies him the most.

Evaluation

Rate the following statement by placing an x beneath the number that best describes the condition in your elementary school. If there are more than one elementary school, each one can be rated separately. Then draw continuous lines through the x's for each school to form a graph. Different colors may be used to distinguish between schools.

1   2   3   4   5

- Children in an art class in the middle and upper grades are working at many different media at the same time.

MUSIC

Vocal and instrumental music have been the two basic divisions of the music world traditionally covered in the elementary school, probably since the first one-room school was built by the settlers who came to the New World. To these two basic subjects, a few other concepts have been added: music appreciation, note reading, biographies of the masters, and the librettos of some of the more well-known operas.

In the primary grades, music is taught by the classroom teacher. Most colleges offering teacher training degrees, require that primary school teachers be able to play the piano with at least mediocre skill, and to be able to lead children in singing.

A specially trained and certified music teacher is hired for the middle and upper grades. In a large elementary school more than one teacher may be hired—one to teach vocal music and the other proficient in instrumental music.

As with the study of art, teaching music to young people should have only one objective in mind: to give them enough background and variety so that music, throughout their life, will bring them pleasure and inspiration.

Evaluation

Rate each of the following statements by placing an x under the appropriate number. If there are more than one elementary school in your community, you may rate each one. Then connect the x's for each school with a continuous line to form a graph for each school. Different colors may be used to distinguish between schools.

                                                                1   2   3   4   5

- Vocal and instrumental music are offered to students in the upper grades.
- A music appreciation course is also offered.

FOREIGN LANGUAGE

Most elementary schools give a survey course in three or four languages: Spanish, French, German, and occasionally Italian. Latin has, over the past twenty or thirty years, gradually died from the elementary curriculum, and in high school it is offered only if enough students request it.

Four or five weeks are devoted to the rudiments of each of the three or four languages, so that by the end of the school year, a student has a basic concept of each one.

The objective of the survey course is to help the seventh and eighth graders determine first, if they want to take a language, and second, which one they prefer to study after they graduate from elementary school and move to the high school.

Other elementary schools, instead of offering a survey course, give an introductory course in each of the languages given in the high school. This type of offering has some disadvantages: (1) Once a student has selected a language it becomes difficult for him to change to another one. (2) The vast majority of students will select Spanish (whether or not this is the language that best suits his needs), because they have heard from a number of sources that this is the easiest language to master.

Evaluation

Rate each of the following statements by placing an x beneath the number that best describes the conditions that exist in your community's school. If there are more than one elementary school, all may be rated individually. Then connect each x with a continuous line for each school, forming a graph. Different colored pencils may be used to distinguish between the various schools.

1 2 3 4 5

- A survey course in foreign languages is given in the upper grades.
- At least three foreign languages are offered.

Chapter Five

THE SECONDARY SCHOOL CURRICULUM

The modern secondary school curriculum covers a wide range of knowledge and skills; it is constructed so as to meet the needs of students whose I.Q.'s range from a low of 80 to a high of 150 or greater. It makes use of many different tools to convey knowledge, understanding, and manual skills to these students. The modern high school curriculum is extensive and it is also viable; it is in constant flux. It is viable because in a dynamic school the courses of study are constantly under review. Change is constant; courses offered one year may be dropped the next and new ones added to take their place.

Much of this change in curriculum and course offering is the result of student interest, or lack of it. In most high schools today at least half of the courses offered are elective and therefore are either accepted by the student body or rejected. Rejected courses fall quickly by the wayside, and are replaced by other courses, often suggested by the students themselves.

American high schools are generally structured so that each subject area is an autonomous entity insofar as what subject matter is to be taught and what courses are to be offered. Heading each department is the chairman or department head, usually a master teacher with an advanced degree. In some schools, in order to conserve money, subjects are linked together under a single department head. The "humanities," for instance, might include the language arts, art, music, and possibly foreign languages or even the social sciences.

In school systems with more than one high school, department heads may be designated as administrators and freed from classroom teaching. They are in charge of their subject area in all the high schools of the district. It is their responsibility not only to be curriculum coordinators, but they are also responsible for the supervision of the teaching staff in their department, for selecting and ordering texts, supplies, and equipment, and for preparing budget requests.

This is not to imply that the teaching staff has no input into formulating and writing the courses of study or selecting texts, or deciding what equipment and supplies are needed. Quite the contrary. A department head invites teachers to assist him in making determinations in all areas of his authority. Many of these decisions are made during meetings of the staff with the department chairman.

For generations, high schools have wrestled with the questions of what should be taught, and no two schools have arrived at the same decisions. Perhaps this is as it should be. The students in a high school in the slums of New York City certainly have different needs from those in the suburbs thirty miles away.

But throughout the years since the first American high school was founded in Boston, certain subjects are still taught, although some changes have been made within the contents of these subjects.

An example is the study of literature in the language arts classes. Pedagogues of past ages recognized the need for each generation to read and to appreciate the classics. The only changes that have taken place over the years lies in the interpretation of what constitutes the "classics."

Back in colonial days the Bible was the primary reading source, along with Virgil and Plato and other writers from the Greeks and Romans. Shakespeare's plays found their way into the classroom in later years, and such novels and poems as *The Lady of the Lake* and *Idylls of the King, The Rime of the Ancient Mariner, Ivanhoe* and *Silas Marner.*

Today the tendency is to teach some of the classics listed above and to add to the classics best sellers from our own times. Excerpts from various books are contained in many "literature" books published for high school English classes, as well as short stories, plays, and poems.

Before a course of study is designed, formulated, and written, the staff who eventually will be teaching it must decide what purpose the course will serve in the lives of the students who take it.

This is part of a far greater problem the high schools of today are facing. There has been a great deal of soul-searching on the part of teachers and administrators who have asked themselves repeatedly over the past years: "Is the curriculum of my high school serving the needs of my students? Is it preparing them for the life they will be facing once they leave here?"

There is no one answer to those questions, because the needs of the students are as diverse as the occupations and the life-styles they choose to enter. A high school that operates a car body shop will serve two purposes: (1) It will prepare a number of students to repair their own cars for the remainder of their lives. (2) It will prepare a select few students to find jobs in auto repair shops.

Then the question arises: Is the four or five hundred thousand dollars that was spent building and equipping this shop and paying for the instructor worth the results? Could the money have been spent better somewhere else?

These same speculative questions can be raised with practically any of the hundreds of courses a large modern high school offers. Why do we teach geometry to the noncollege bound student? Why do we teach it to the college bound student who plans to become a doctor? Or an electrical engineer? Will they ever make use of any of the knowledge they acquired in the course that cost them an hour a day for a year? How about a student who plans on becoming an architect? Is geometry more closely allied to his future needs?

Latin has been taught for generations, yet it is spoken no where in the world today except in church masses. Yet proponents of the language insist that Latin forms the basis for English, and that by learning Latin, students will have a good background for understanding their own tongue. And opponents reply: "And why not use the time learning Latin and apply it to a better understanding of English? Why go all around Robin Hood's barn to achieve the same objective?"

Therefore, when a course of study is written, it contains several sentences called "objectives" which seek to justify why the course should exist and what it will do for the students who take it.

In the *general* objectives the writers will state what overall results they wish to attain, as in this curriculum guide for a course in "Child Psychology and Child Development":

1. To promote knowledge and understanding about how children develop and why they act as they do.

2. To develop mental and physical skills and abilities in dealing with young children.

3. To help the students in the class develop attitudinal changes toward the care and management of younger children.

4. To take care of individual differences in the students who attend the class.

5. To list a number of learning activities which will promote the other objectives listed herein.

6. To provide an evaluation of how successful the course has been in bringing about these objectives and the specific objectives listed below.

The *Specific objectives* for the same course contained the following:

1. To study in depth the textbook, *Child Growth and Development.*

2. To visit classes in the elementary school. During these visits each high school student in the class will pick out a child in the elementary class for study. At the end of the course, the student will write a paper on the results of the study and what the student has learned.

3. To invite preschool children to the high school for two hours each morning for several weeks.

4. To divide the class into three groups and assign each a topic for research and discussion, followed by an oral report to the rest of the class. Topics to be assigned: (1) the backward child, socially and mentally, (2) the rebellious child, (3) the showoff child.

5. To evaluate the success of the course.

Although such statements as those given in the general and specific objectives do not assure posterity that the course will fulfill all the demands of its students during the years to come, it does guarantee, to a degree, that the course will at least meet the needs of some students. Requiring that each course of study contain objectives should cut from the curriculum such nonsense courses as basket weaving, doll collecting, and the like, which have actually found their way into a few school curricula.

One way that many schools have answered the question: "Are the courses is this school serving the needs of our students?" is by increasing the number of electives and decreasing the number of required courses. This method turns the responsibility over to the student. In effect the school is saying, "Look, we're offering you all these hundred or so courses. Now, surely, out of that many you should be able to find the ones that suit your future needs." That logic, of course, assumes that a teenager knows what his future needs are. At that age, unfortunately, many haven't yet decided what career they will enter.

Probably you have talked to high school graduates who have been away from the classroom for several years, and you have probably asked them what courses have been useful to them since graduation and which ones were a waste of time, in their estimation. In my experience "hands-on" courses like personal typewriting, bookkeeping, certain shops, writing workshops, and the like were listed in the favorable column, while courses like U.S. History I and II, geometry, Latin, algebra, and English literature were given thumbs down.

All parents of high school students, or parents whose sons or daughters will be entering high school in the near future, should borrow copies of the schools courses of study in the subjects which their children are now taking or soon will be taking and read them from a critical point of view. They make interesting reading, and there is probably no better method of gaining an insight into the heart of the school's philosophy and thinking than through the courses of study—the curriculum of the school which in all essence *is* the school!

The remainder of this chapter will examine each of the various departments which make up a modern high school and will point out what parents should look for in evaluating these subjects areas.

Evaluation

Rate each statement below by placing an x below the number which best describes the conditions in your community's high school. Then connect all the x's with a continuous line to form a graph.

                                                        1 2 3 4 5

- The high school in my community has a course of study for every subject.
- The courses of study in my community's high school are constantly under review.
- New courses are offered every year; courses with few students are dropped.
- Each department in my community's high school has a department head as an overseer.
- The curriculum of my community's high school meets the needs of *all* its students.
- The courses of study I have examined contain:
    General objectives
    Specific objectives
    Course content
    Audio visual references
    Texts to be used
    Units of work
    Means of evaluating student achievement

LANGUAGE ARTS

Educators agree that the language arts curriculum consists of two main subjects: the study of literature and the development of good written and oral skills. But that's where the concurrence ends. What topics should be included under each of these two main headings is and has been in disagreement for the past fifty years. And further controversy exists over *how* the subject should be taught.

Let's discuss the first of the two main headings: literature. In the language arts classes that I have visited during my tenure as an administrator, I have been depressed by the amount of time that teachers give to the study of literature to the exclusion of the other language arts subjects. It isn't difficult to guess why this is so. Teaching literature is far more enjoyable than teaching grammar or composition.

Literature classes usually begin by the teacher making a controversial statement about a character in the book that is under consideration, or perhaps asking a question as to why a character acted as he did. The remainder of the class period consists of the teacher acting as a moderator while the students toss the question back and forth.

The teacher spends a comfortable hour at his desk with the students doing most of the work.

This is not to say that the classics and other books of literary merit shouldn't be addressed in this manner. The complaint comes, because it is a practice that goes on for weeks, sometimes months, as one book after another is dissected, masticated, and digested. Is it any wonder that so many of our high school graduates do little book reading during their adult lives?

One book a year which has been critiqued to death is sufficient to impress on any youngster how a work of art can be chopped to pieces.

Another method of teaching literature, which some schools have adopted, is the core curriculum. The idea in core curriculum is to marry an allied subject from a different department with a piece of literature in the language arts department and hope the marriage doesn't end in divorce before the end of the term. Example: students in the social studies department are studying the American Indian. Would the English Department like to study *Hiawatha* so the two classes can work together on the same subject, and have the combined language arts and social studies classes reaping the benefits of both teachers working together as a team?

The idea sounds reasonable, but unfortunately, in my experience, it seldom works out as the planners had expected. In the example above, the students in the social studies class probably resent what they consider an intrusion into their subject area, one they had not bargained for when they elected the course. The literature student may gain some background material for understanding the poem better, but in all likelihood, the Indian tribe discussed by the social studies teacher is far removed geographically from Hiawatha's.

This entire marriage is artificial. The weakness of the core curriculum concept occurs because it is difficult to find two topics from different departments that are close enough in subject content to be teachable as a single unit.

Much variation among high schools occurs when one examines the titles of the books which are placed on the student reading list. There are a number of the "old" classics which are fairly universally taught in American high schools: Shakespeare's plays, the *Iliad* and the *Odyssey*, Dickens's *Christmas Carol* and *A Tale of Two Cities*, perhaps Hawthorne's *Scarlet Letter*, and some of the longer poems like "Evangeline" and "Hiawatha" by American authors. Added to the classics are many books by modern authors, some of them sufficiently controversial in nature to result in "book burnings" by boards of education after the public outcry becomes loud enough.

Which books a school selects is probably immaterial as long as they are a representative sampling of the best of the old and the new. Students should have leeway in selecting which books they choose to read. To accomplish this, language arts departments publish a "suggested book list," and each incoming freshman is given a copy which he is instructed to follow throughout his high school career. A mandatory number of books to be read per semester is then established by the language arts department, and a file is kept on each student.

In addition to reading the book, the student is generally required to write a report on his reading.

The books contained in the reading list are in addition to the core books taught in class and discussed above.

The second division of subject matter contained in the language arts course of study, the development of good writing and oral skills, in my estimation, deserves the greater weight in time and effort by the teaching staff, particularly the development of acceptable writing skills.

Unfortunately, Americans are noted for their inability to communicate effectively in their native tongue. It has been estimated that over one-half of American high school graduates have writing skills equal to or below that required of a sixth grader. The most common complaint coming from business and industry in regard to the high school graduates whom they have interviewed for jobs is that these young men and women cannot read or write.

Colleges, too, find the reading and writing ability of many incoming freshmen below the standards needed for success in many of the courses required during the first year. Subsequently, either one of two alternatives results: (1) the incoming freshman flunks out after the first semester and either abandons hopes of a college career or goes to a junior college for a year or two, or (2) the college institutes noncredit courses in reading and writing improvement. In other words, the college takes on the responsibility abandoned by the high school.

There has been a great deal of study (and controversy) on the most effective way of teaching writing skills. In the past, the method in greatest use consisted of classes which taught formal grammar, distinct and separate from all other related subjects. Week after week, sentences were parsed and students filled in thousands of blanks using the correct form of the pronoun, the correct verb form, underlining subjects once, predicates twice, objects three times, indirect objects four times.

One teacher spent three weeks teaching a class of students, most of whom had no intentions of extending their education beyond high school, all about subjunctive mood, and another two weeks trying to get her class to conjugate a number of irregular verbs. As one of the students left the classroom, he was overheard to say to a buddy of his, "She don't explain things too good."

And what are the results when grammar is taught in isolation? In every case, except in classes where the students have a high I.Q., teachers found little or no carryover from the formal grammar teaching to the written work. Grammar and correct usage should be taught as an integrated part of the writing process, as explained in the previous chapter, "The Elementary School Curriculum."

It should be pointed out, too, that the English language, as spoken by Americans, is undergoing rather rapid change toward simplification. Pick up any newspaper today, or listen to the radio or television announcers, most of whom pride themselves on their ability to speak correctly, and you will get a good idea of how widespread this change is.

For example, the word "whom" is dying from the language. "As", when introducing a clause, is being replaced by like: Correct, "do *as* I tell you to," not "do *like* I tell you to." Or the advertisement catch-phrase which may well have been the beginning of the demise for "as" as an adverb: "Winston tastes good like a cigarette should."

Simplification of a language is not necessarily something to be fought as long as the simplification does not result in ambiguity or confusion of meaning. In the cases cited above, this is not the case, and if the objective form of who is dropped from the language, teachers will find it far less difficult to teach the objective case of pronouns.

Evaluation

Rate each of the following statements by placing an x below the number which best describes conditions in your community's high school. Then connect all the x's with a continuous line to form a graph.

1 2 3 4 5

- Teachers give proportionate time to the teaching of literature and to the development of good writing and oral skills.
- A representative selection of books from the masters and from modern literature is included in the Required Reading List.
- Book reports are required.
- Grammar and good usage are taught as an integral part of the writing process.
- Teachers correct all written work and require that it be rewritten, making corrections.

SOCIAL STUDIES

If you were to examine the social studies courses of study for a number of secondary schools throughout the country, you would find that the overall objectives are fairly similar in all the schools. The following is an example of one such set of objectives:

1. To understand the history of the human race and appreciate the problems facing each culture that preceded our own, and the hopes and achievements that the people of these cultures lived for.

2. To develop good citizenship.

3. To understand other cultures and subcultures in present day society.

4. To develop the ability to think critically and logically.

5. To understand the complex nature of today's social, economic and political problems and to be familiar with the various measures which have and are being used to solve them.

The social studies departments of all high schools have undergone tremendous change during the past fifty years. The scope and dimensions of the subject content, as well as the number and types of courses offered to students, have expanded vastly. Following is a typical course offering for a high school prior to World War II:

United States History I
United States History II
World History
Civics
The Egyptians, the Greeks, and the Romans

Now compare this with a partial list of the course offerings from a recent high school curriculum guide:

Our Vanishing Ozone Layer
Civilization's Trash and What To Do with It
Hitler and World War II
Knights and Ladies of Medieval Days
Problems in the Near East
The United States Congress
Psychology I and II
Adolescent Psychology
Abnormal Psychology
Teen-age Problems and How to Cope with Them
Anthropology
Religions of the World
The Civil War
United States Expansion to the Pacific
Philosophy I and II
Ancient Civilizations
Prehistoric Man
The Age of the Dinosaur
The Iron Age
Types of Governments Throughout History
The Dawn of Modern Technology
The History of Space Travel

All of the above courses were offered as electives. Most were of one semester duration; a few were full year courses, and a small percentage were quarter semester courses. All students were required to take a total of fifteen credit hours, including the two required courses, American History I and II taken in their junior and senior years, and mandated by state law.

If more than one section of a course had to be scheduled because of heavy student enrollment, the students were grouped homogeneously, and the curriculum content for the class which contained the under-achievers was modified to meet their ability level. Guidance counselors, while conferring with students during scheduling sessions for the following year, steered each student into only those electives for which the student had the capabilities to succeed.

To teach the subjects contained in the high school curriculum of fifty years ago, a teacher needed to be proficient in only a narrow field of knowledge. Not so with the modern high school teacher. As a result, many high schools are finding it difficult to locate teachers who are proficient enough for the school to offer such a wide range of subjects. Occasionally, it has been found, the curriculum is determined not by the needs of the students but by the interests and fields of knowledge of its teaching staff.

Evaluation

Rate each of the following statements by placing an x under the appropriate number. Then connect the x's with a continuous line to form a graph.

1 2 3 4 5

- The social studies department has a set of objectives which set forth the goals of the department.
- The social studies department offers a wide range of courses.
- Most of the courses are semester in length.
- All courses are elective except those required by state law.
- Courses are determined by student interest and needs and not by teacher preference and range of knowledge.

SCIENCE

Like social studies, the science departments of our high schools have broadened the scope of inquiry contained in their courses of study. A revolution occurred with the onset of the age of "sputniks." The American people looked to our high schools and colleges to produce the scientists our nation needed in order to compete and exceed the accomplishments of the Russians.

The science curriculum of the American high school has not been without criticism, some of it just and some the result of the hysteria which followed Russia's achievements in space. Fortunately, much of this criticism has subsided somewhat since the United States has made significant achievements in its own space program.

However, parents might look at their own high schools and ask the following questions:

Is there evidence that the science curriculum has become "gadget" infested—students building models and projects on which much of their grade is determined? Are "science fairs" taking over to the detriment of basic learning, particularly in classes for the overachiever?

Is at least a part of the chemistry curriculum, technology-oriented? Are students directed toward the applications of chemistry in such fields as metallurgy, ceramics, dyes, textiles, fertilizers, plastics, perfumes, fuels, inks, synthetics, and explosives?

Are students made aware of the basic compounds out of the over half million identified to date?

Has biology become more of a "hobby" than a science? Does the course reveal (1) the progression of life from the molecule through the organelle, to the cell, to tissue, to the organ, to the organism itself and then on to the species and the community, (2) the pros and cons of evolution, (3) ecological and behavioral phenomena?

Does the general science course for the noncollege-bound student give him an understanding of the physical world into which he has been born, how it affects his life, and how mankind's actions affect the future of his world?

The science curriculum must be constructed so that it takes care of the needs of roughly three groups of students: (1) those going on to careers in a field of science or a related field; (2) those who plan to continue their education beyond high school and need a fundamental, basic background in biology, chemistry, physics and the earth sciences; (3) those who will terminate their education on or before they graduate from high school.

Group One. The number of courses that can be offered for students planning a career in the sciences will depend to a large extent on the enrollment of the high school. Small schools cannot afford to offer in-depth subjects because the number of students enrolled in these advanced subjects would be insufficient to warrant the costs involved.

In all high schools the following basic subjects should be offered: Chemistry I, Biology I, Physics I. Larger high schools should also include Organic Chemistry, Biology II, and Physics II.

Besides the basics, these courses should also focus on the technology of each field and how the science is applied to modern living. There has been considerable speculation as to why the United States is falling behind in technological advancements, and many have aimed their criticism at the high schools and colleges of the nation, citing that these schools concentrate too heavily on the pure sciences to the exclusion of technological applications.

Group Two. For students going to college but not planning to major in science or a closely-related subject, it is recommended that a survey course of at least a year be offered. This course should concentrate on the four main subdivisions of the science curriculum—physics, chemistry, biology, and earth sciences and should stress the basics of each of the subjects.

Group Three. For students not planning to attend college, a one-year course, general science, should be required at the freshman level and should emphasize the role of science in the student's everyday life, how it affects his health, his livelihood, and his well-being.

The course, as far as possible, should be a "hands-on" course. There should be many simple experiments the students can perform. They should have access to microscopes and slides, have experience operating a telescope during several nighttime class periods, and should perform experiments in the laboratory that will acquaint them with the basic laws of physics, chemistry, and biology. Field trips should also be included in the curriculum.

The instructor should make frequent use of the overhead projector, motion pictures, video cassettes, and the slide projector to supplement the text.

Evaluation

Rate each of the following statements by placing an x beneath the appropriate number. Then connect the x's with a continuous line to form a graph.

1 2 3 4 5

- The science program is not "gadget"-infested.
- The chemistry course of study is technology oriented to some degree.
- The science curriculum contains sufficient courses for those students planning a career in a science-related industry.
- The science curriculum contains sufficient courses for those going on to college but not entering a science-related subject.

1   2   3   4   5

- The science curriculum contains a general science course for students not planing to attend college.
- All courses have at least one laboratory period per week; college-bound students have seven periods of science per week, two of which are lab periods; all others have five.

MATHEMATICS

The role of the elementary school is to give the students who enter high school a sound foundation in the fundamentals of mathematics. These include proficiency in adding, subtracting, multiplying, and dividing whole numbers, fractions, and decimals.

The job of the high school is to build on this foundation and train each student according to his ability, as well as to prepare him for his future employment.

One of the problems the high schools faces is a student's inability, at this stage in his life, to know with any degree of certainty what line of work he wishes to engage in after he finishes his education. However, intelligence tests, past grades, and interests expressed to counselors during interviews can help school officials succeed to some degree in deciding what type of mathematics each student should study.

Students may be scheduled into one of three categories: (1) Students who plan to become shopkeepers, clerks, stenographers, construction workers, and similar jobs, and (2) Engineers, mathematicians, researchers, statisticians, and physicists, and (3) bankers, tellers, bookkeepers, and certain computer operators.

For students entering the first category the following units of work are samplings of the type of exercises which seem appropriate for their needs: keeping simple books; preparing invoices; tax preparations, long form; obtaining and completing various government forms; balancing a checkbook, real estate transactions; figuring interest payments, both personal and business; and computer programming. All of these units of work rely on some form of mathematical computation.

For students entering the second category the following courses seem appropriate: Algebra I, Algebra II, Plane Geometry, Solid Geometry, Trigonometry, Differential Calculus, Integral Calculus, and Basic Computer programming (preferably in Pascal).

Students selecting the third category should consider such subjects as Bookkeeping I and II, Basic Statistics, and Record Keeping. Often the curriculum for this group of students is developed and operated by the business department with assistance from the mathematics department and contains related subjects such as typing and stenography.

Recently the National Council of Teachers of Mathematics announced fifty-four curriculum and evaluation standards to make sure that America's students could explore and reason as well as to add and subtract. Under these new guidelines, students would be exposed to less rote memorization, more computers and calculators, and cooperative teamwork instead of one-on-one competition. More practical applications of mathematics were suggested: designing a bird house, building a scale model of the solar system, creating graphs from statistics supplied by newspaper items of current trends.

American children do well in international competitions on basic arithmetical skills, but poorly when required to apply these skills to mathematical principles. "Only about one-half of American 17 year olds can say whether 87 percent of 10 is less than 10, greater than 10 or equal to 10," said John Dossy, chairman of National Council of Teachers of Mathematics's Standards Implementation Commission. "Only half can figure out how much carpet is needed to cover a floor or calculate the probability of a simple event," he added. "Applied mathematics is not just for a couple of geniuses in the country," said Sally Ride, a Stanford University physicist and former astronaut.

Developers of this new approach to the teaching of mathematics emphasized that many students find math an extremely dull subject. They concluded, therefore, that rote practice and drills should not be completely abandoned, but should not dominate the classroom period either.

Also included in the guidelines is the requirement that the teaching of mathematics be kept in the context of everyday life, with such problems as grocery shopping, motorcycle races, used car purchases, savings accounts, pulse rates, and taste tests.

Evaluation

Rate each of the following statements by placing an x beneath the appropriate number. Then connect the x's with a continuous line to form a graph.

1   2   3   4   5

- The school offers the following courses for the student who plans to follow a career which requires higher mathematics:

Algebra I

Algebra II

Plane Geometry

Solid Geometry

Trigonometry

Differential Calculus

Integral Calculus

Computer Programming

- The school offers courses for the business-oriented student such as bookkeeping, advanced bookkeeping, stenography, etc.
- The school offers courses for students who will work in banks and CPA offices

FOREIGN LANGUAGE

Much criticism has been leveled against the foreign language departments of this country's high schools and colleges. The primary criticism is that, after four or more years of studying a language, many students have difficulty speaking and writing the language as fluently as would be expected. Particular difficulty is experienced by many students because of faulty pronunciation.

The use of a language laboratory is a partial solution to the problem of poor enunciation. Here a student will (1) hear a word, phrase, or sentence spoken correctly; speak into a microphone and say the word, sentence, or phrase himself; and listen back to both the original words and then his own so that he may make a comparison. If he isn't satisfied with his first attempt, he may rewind the tape and have a second go at it.

If a school does not have a language laboratory, the next best method of teaching the language is to have the classroom teacher insist that not one word of English is spoken after students enter the room. All conversation and explanations are carried on in the language being taught. Games are played, plays and skits produced, stories written and read to the class, newspapers read aloud—all in the tongue of the country being studied.

The study of foreign languages has never been a top priority with the American public. Because our country is isolated geographically from much of the world, and because English has to a great extent become an international language, Americans have never felt any great compelling need to know another language. Further, tourists have found that no matter where they go in the world, there is always someone who can speak English and translate for them.

For a long time—from the turn of the century until after World War II—the main reason why a student selected and studied a language was because he needed it in order to be admitted to college. Today, fewer and fewer colleges are requiring a language as a prerequisite for admission unless the student expects to take up a subject for which a foreign language is essential.

Those entering the diplomatic service, engineers working abroad, and sales representatives in the import-export business are a few of the types of jobs that require expertise in speaking a foreign language. But when a youngster is in his high-school years, he has no inkling as to his fitness for such a position perhaps ten or fifteen years down the road, and therefore cannot make any rational judgment as to whether he should take a language, and if so, which one.

Most larger high schools offer at least three years, preferably four years of French, German, Spanish, and Latin. A few have added Russian. Why these languages? Probably because traditionally they are the languages that have always been in the high school curriculum, and because these are the languages that large numbers of teachers have been trained to teach. But what about Arabic? Japanese? Portuguese? Chinese? These languages have taken a front seat in world affairs today, and many of them certainly are more useful than Latin in today's society.

Evaluation

Rate each of the following statements by placing an x beneath the appropriate number. Then connect the x's with a continuous line to form a graph.

1 2 3 4 5

• The high school offers students *at least* three years of the following languages:

German

Spanish

French

Latin

Russian

Italian

- The school offers students the use of a language laboratory for
  at least one period a week.
- Foreign language is offered as an elective.

BUSINESS EDUCATION

The curriculum of the business education department is aimed primarily at the students who are planning to enter some phase of the business world after graduation from high school, or who plan to take up business administration or a related subject in college. However, a minor role of this department is to provide a few courses for those students who wish to improve their proficiency in typing, for instance, or who want a course in personal money management.

For these students such courses as personal typing, personal record keeping, stenography for the college bound, and basic computer operation are offered.

For the business student: typing I and II, stenography I and II, bookkeeping I and II, computer operation I and II, retail sales, cashiering, work-study programs, retail display, salesmanship, jobs in the service industries, marketing, stock market and investing, preparing for real estate sales, filing methods, office management, and business letter writing are examples of just a few of the types of courses offered by a modern high school's business department.

Evaluation

Rate each of the following statements by placing an x beneath the appropriate number. Then connect the x's with a continuous line to form a graph.

1   2   3   4   5

- The majority of courses offered are aimed at training students to
  enter the business world after graduation.
- Some courses are offered for the college-bound.
- A work-study program is offered by the business department
  (see On the Job Training under INNOVATIVE PROGRAMS at
  the conclusion of this chapter).

ART

Because most art expression in the United States today is oriented toward commercial use, it seems logical that a good part of the art curriculum in the high school should lead toward some utilitarian purpose.

Therefore, for the student who is seriously considering a career in art, it is important that early in his high school days he becomes acquainted with the many job opportunities open to him in advertising, interior decorating, magazine and book illustrating, textile design, and natural and artificial flower arrangement, to name just a few.

During the freshman year, it is recommended that a survey course be given in which there is a wide sampling of how art is used in industry and commerce. From such a course the student will become familiar with the many avenues open to him in commercial art, and thus enable him to make a more judicious choice of the field he wishes to enter by the time he leaves high school.

Following the survey course, all art-oriented students should be presented with a list of minicourses, some semester in length, some half semester. From this list he then selects those subjects in which his interests lie—two semester courses or four half-semester. The following is a partial list from a current high school art curriculum:

Painting and Drawing	Architectural Design
Ceramics	Line Drawing
Sculpturing	Lettering
Weaving	Wood Carving
Advertising Art	Cubism
Store Window Decorating	Surrealism
Commercial Art	Textile Design
Silk Screen	Interior Decorating
Linoleum Block	Flower Display
Commercial Posters	Book Illustrating
Stain Glass	Wall Paper Design
Art History	Dress Designing
Art Appreciation	

An examination of this partial list of minicourses reveals that there are courses for the student (1) who is planning a career in commercial art, (2) courses for those students who are primarily interested in art for pleasure and as a means of self-satisfaction, and (3) courses for the student who turns to art as a hobby.

Once the basics of each course has been taught and mastered, complete freedom of expression and choice is a must. Most of these courses lend themselves to use of slides, films, filmstrips, video tapes, and actual examples. They should be available on a one-on-one basis at a time when the student is ready for them or when the instructor feels that a viewing would assist a student overcome some difficulty he is encountering.

Evaluation

Rate the following statements by placing an x beneath the appropriate number. Then connect the x's with a continuous line to form a graph.

1 2 3 4 5

- Commercial art is emphasized by the art department in its curriculum offerings.
- A survey course is offered for freshmen.
- A wide range of subjects is offered.
- Semester and half-semester courses make up the majority of courses.
- Students may take courses in other subject areas by meshing them with those in the art department.
- Courses for hobby enthusiasts are offered.

MUSIC

Music instruction, as well as music for pleasure, has been a part of the secondary scene for generations. In the old days, students attended "chapel" at least once a week, and a good portion of the program was devoted to group singing. Early curricula consisted mainly of vocal instruction, the teaching of piano, a study of the masters, and perhaps a string ensemble. Much of the music was religious in nature and rarely, if ever, included a study of the folk or "popular" music of the day.

Today's high school curriculum is much broader and more liberal in its content, ranging from the study of African music to Be-bop, the theory being that there is no one music that is best for all.

A number of short courses, such as described above for the art department, is considered superior to full-year courses which contain a wide range of subject matter. These mini-courses in music can be "meshed" with those of the art department's, if such is the desire of a student. In fact, many schools mesh minicourses in art, music, home economics, and industrial arts, thus catering to a wide range of interests among their students.

The following is a partial list of minicourses offered in many present-day high schools:

Music of the Masters	Religious Music
The Romanticists	The Concerto
Rock Music	The Materials of Music
Forming Your Own Band	Scores from Movies
History of Jazz	Intervals and Triads

American Folk Music
Composing Techniques
Reading Music
Beginning Piano
Beginning Organ
Opera
The Symphony
Conducting an Orchestra or Band

Rhythm in Music
Motif, Melody, and Harmony
Modern Musical Instruments
Marching Band }
Orchestra }
Choir } half or full year courses
Dance Band }

Here again, as in the art curriculum, courses are offered to meet the needs of any student who is contemplating a career in the music field, as well as for the student who has a casual interest in the subject.

Evaluation

Rate each of the following statements by placing an x beneath the appropriate number. Then connect the x's with a continuous line to form a graph.

1 2 3 4 5

- Courses offered by the music department cover a wide range including modern music.
- Courses are semester or half-semester in length and may be meshed with other departments.
- The school services at least a marching band and a choir.
- Courses are offered for the student who wishes to pursue a career in music and for the student who seeks to improve his enjoyment of music.

HOME ECONOMICS

Educators of thirty or forty years ago might look aghast to see both boys and girls enrolled in home economics, industrial arts, and physical education classes. Yet this is the common practice in high schools today. Because most of these courses are electives, any student may sign up for them as long as they meet the prerequisites.

The following minicourses are representative of those offered in the nation's high schools. Again, these may be meshed with art, music, and industrial arts courses and are semester or half-semester in length.

Child Management
Child Growth and Development
Preparing for Marriage
Home Management

Sewing for Beginners
Advanced Sewing
Sewing Apparel
Food Shopping

Home Finances
Cooking for a Few
Cooking for Large Groups
Food Preparation
Buying a Home

Clothing Design
Sewing Curtains and Drapes
Child Psychology
So You're Going to Have a Baby
Going Steady

Evaluation

Rate each of the following statements by placing an x beneath the appropriate number. Then connect the x's with a continuous line to form a graph.

1 2 3 4 5

- Boys and girls are permitted to enroll in home economic courses.
- Courses include as the minimum the following subject areas:

    Several kinds of cooking classes

    Various sewing classes

    Child-rearing classes

    Child psychology classes

    Home management classes

- Courses are elective.
- Courses are semester, and half semester in length.
- Courses may be meshed with other subject areas such as music, art, and industrial arts.

INDUSTRIAL ARTS

The industrial arts curriculum is made up of courses in six main areas: wood, metal, electric, auto, printing, and drafting. Not all high schools can afford all six shops; the number of students enrolled in the school is usually the main determining factor.

Other factors which may affect the number and size of the shops are the needs of the community in which the school is located, the background and prejudices of the board members who approve the building plans, and the wealth of the community supplying the funds to construct the building. (Shops are usually one of the first classrooms in a building to be "axed" when economies must be made.)

Following is a partial list of minicourses offered by the industrial arts department:

Drafting. Home design, Designing a garage, Public park layouts, Laying out a golf course, Planning an office building, Designing staircases,

Types of roof structures, Windows and where to place them, Structural design, and Steel girder use.

Wood. Home repairs, Furniture finishing, Furniture building, Caning, Basics of home construction, Roofing, Hanging a door, Cabinet building, Laying a floor, Ceramic tiling, and Building bookshelves.

Metal. Jewelry making, Copper ornaments for the home, Metal lathe work, Sheet metal basics, Home repairs, Installing sewers, Installing water pipes, Installing air conditioning ducts, Installing forced hot air heat, and Installing exhaust systems.

Electric. Wiring a lamp, Basics of house wiring, Radio repair, Elements of TV repair, D.C. Current circuits, Principles of A.C. circuits, Home electrical repairs, and Small appliance repairs.

Auto. Tire maintenance and repair, Automobile electrical systems repair, Repairing your car's fuel system, Replacing brake linings, Beginners' auto repair, Small engine repair, Repairing your car's exhaust system, Welding, and Repairing and painting auto body damage.

Printing and Photography. Principles of offset printing, Letterpress printing, Personal photography, Plate making for offset printing, Commercial photography, Printing the small newspaper, Color developing, Stationery and business card printing, and Circular printing.

Evaluation

Rate each of the following statements by placing an x beneath the number which best describes the conditions in your community's high school. Then draw a continuous line through all the x's to form a graph.

                                                                1 2 3 4 5

- The high school in my community offers courses in the following industrial arts subjects:

    Drafting

    Wood

    Metal

    Electricity

    Automobile repair and body work

    Printing and photography

    (Schools with small enrollments should make allowances if fewer than the six subjects listed above are included in the curriculum.)

- Students may make their own selection of courses in industrial arts.
- The school offers a series of minicourses in industrial arts.

INNOVATIVE PROGRAMS

One of the main duties of the administration of a high school is to keep a constant eye on the curriculum of the various departments, and to confer with the department heads in an effort to improve what is being taught.

Improvement includes: (1) dropping courses which are not filling the needs of the student body, (2) devising and writing new courses of study, (3) revising present courses, (4) promoting interaction between departments when it is indicated, (5) changing textbooks, and (6) trying new and innovative programs to improve the curriculum.

For the past thirty years the federal government has been making grants to local school districts in an effort to improve the quality of education in the nation's schools. The theory behind these grants was based on the belief that if money was available, innovative programs would be forthcoming.

While this belief was partially true, a number of districts in their haste to get in on the "gravy train" hurriedly concocted programs which either did not work or did not attack a problem of sufficient importance to warrant the expenditure.

Out of the thousands of federal programs a number emerged which were of sufficient merit to be duplicated in other school districts. The following programs were either a result of federal spending or were in existence at the time the government entered the educational field.

Team Teaching. The ultimate in team teaching requires an open-area school (also called the open classroom), but hybrid versions may be conducted in a conventional building. The staff is divided into three or more teams and students separated homogeneously by ability.

Each team of teachers has a leader who coordinates the activities of the group and is responsible for all team progress. Teacher aides and volunteers may also be a part of the team.

Each team of teachers has a specialist in social studies, mathematics, language arts, and science. These specialists present the material contained in the course of study pertaining to their subject-area. The subjects are so constructed that each of the four major disciplines plays an equal part in the presentation and evaluation.

On-the-Job Training. A student spends half the school day in school attending classes in the required subjects and the afternoon at a job training program. Although the student is usually paid for his work, the primary objective of the course is to help him develop the skills he needs to advance in the field of his chosen work. The employer guarantees that he will provide the necessary training, and the school oversees the student and counsels him on a regular basis.

Accelerated Course. Accelerated courses are available for the fast learner who is mature enough to work on his own much of the time. The work is so designed that the student may move ahead as rapidly as he is capable of. All work is individualized instruction.

Individualized Instruction. Capable students work on their own from a "work sheet," divided into units of work. Each unit of work contains an objective which the student works toward, reference material, audiovisual referrals and an evaluative criteria. When the student has satisfactorily completed one unit of work, he moves on to the next until he has completed the entire course of study. He is then tested on the entire body of knowledge.

Advanced Placement. Superior students are permitted to begin their college career while they are seniors in high school. They carry both the high school courses and college courses at the same time, usually attending college in late afternoon. The college credit they earn is usually applicable toward their college degree.

Bilingual Education is instituted to assist students who do not have an adequate command of the English language to attend regular classes. In these special classes, both English and the student's native tongue are spoken. The objective is to teach the subject matter of the course and at the same time to assist the student in learning English so he may be mainstreamed into regular classes.

Contract Learning. Contract learning is somewhat similar to individualized instruction. The student "contracts" with the teacher to do a specified amount of individualized work, and then proceeds on his own, using work sheets to direct him in his activities.

All-Year School. Educators have long been concerned about the length of time school buildings remain unoccupied during the summer months. To overcome this wasted time, the school year is extended to twelve months, and is divided into four equal quarters. A student (and his parents) selects any three sequential quarters.

In order for this program to be successful, the building must be air conditioned, and a sufficient number of students must have selected the quarter term which falls during the summer months.

Programs for the Educable and Trainable. All states require that schools provide special classes for the mentally handicapped, designated as educable (slightly handicapped) and trainable (severely handicapped). This is a specialized field and requires in-depth training for its teachers who usually possess at least a master's degree.

Programs for the Blind, Deaf, Hard of Hearing, Orthopedically Handicapped, Those with Speech Defects and other Handicaps. This is also a specialized field and requires specially trained teachers.

Programmed Instruction is an individualized type of learning in which all units of work are contained either on a computer, a teaching machine or on video tape. The student proceeds through the entire course on his own, testing himself at the end of each unit of work.

R.O.T.C. (Reserve Officer's Training Corps) This program originated in the colleges and filtered down to the high school where it has become a very popular program among a certain group of boys and girls. In the program the students receive military training.

Study Abroad Plan. A plan usually implemented by the language arts department to help students acquire proficiency in the language of the country they visit. It is customarily carried on during the summer vacation. The students often reside with families in the foreign country, and therefore learn the customs and mores of the country as well as its language.

Evaluation

Rate each of the following statements by placing an x beneath the appropriate number. Then connect the x's with a continuous line to form a graph.

1 2 3 4 5

- The high school in my community revises its curriculum regularly.
- The high school in my community revises the courses it offers each year.
- The high school in my community has innovative programs.
- The high school in my community has classes for the mentally retarded and the handicapped.

Chapter Six

ELEMENTARY SCHOOL STAFF

Of all the components that make up a modern school, none is more important than the teachers and specialized personnel that make up its faculty. A good teacher usually turns out good scholars, and one poor teacher can affect a student's behavior, his attitude toward learning, and his achievement for the remaining years that he stays in school.

Studies have shown that over 75 percent of the students who drop out of high school before graduation, had an inferior teacher at some time earlier in their educational career, usually in the first four or five years.

A typical American public school is comprised of two groups of employees—administration and staff. The administration might be compared to the executive branch of industry; the staff to the workers. This chapter will deal solely with the staff and will focus on the elementary school. Chapter Seven will discuss the secondary school staff.

Before examining the elementary school staff something should be said about class size. It would not be fair to compare a teacher who has a class of twenty students with one who has thirty or thirty-five. Studies have been made to determine the maximum size of a class in various grade levels, over which the teacher will find it difficult to give each student the individual help and assistance he or she needs. These maxima are as follows: kindergarten—20 (28 with a lay assistant), grades one through six—25 (preferably fewer in the lower grades, perhaps one or two more in the upper grades).

The elementary school is not nearly as complicated as the secondary school insofar as the variety and duties of its staff. A typical elementary school usually consists of the following specialists: (1) classroom teaching staff, divided roughly into four groups—preschool and kindergarten, lower grades (one through three), middle grades (three through five), and upper grades (five through seven; grade eight if there is no junior high or middle school in the district); (2) librarian, now referred to as a media specialist; (3) atypical teachers; (4) physical education teachers; (5) nurse; (6) guidance; (7) clerks and secretaries.

CLASSROOM TEACHERS

1. **Training.** Today's teacher should have at least a bachelor's degree from an accredited college. In addition, the teacher should have gone through a period of apprenticeship, usually referred to as practice teaching.

There is considerable controversy as to which type of college better prepares a teacher—a liberal arts college or a teachers' training college. The teachers' colleges tend to overburden the student with a preponderance of teacher-training courses to the detriment of courses in the subjects which the teacher will teach (the three R's plus geography, social studies, art, music, and composition for elementary school teachers). A few of these "education courses," as they are referred to, are probably beneficial, such as child psychology, adolescent psychology, classroom management, preparation of lesson plans, and managing extracurricular activities. But most administrators now believe that a superior teacher is born a teacher, and if he or she doesn't have the required talent, no courses are going to help to any great extent.

Sadly enough, a degree today does not always mean that a graduate is literate. There is the classic example of the fifth-grade teacher with a *master's* degree who sent the following message home to a parent: "Scott is droping in his studies he acts as if he don't care. Scott wont pass in his assignment at all, he had a poem to learn and he fell to do it."

2. **Competency.** Because the classroom teacher is the single-most important element in the education of our children, the competency of each teacher is of vital importance in evaluating a school.

How is a competent teacher defined? A competent teacher is one who has mastered his subject matter and is able to inspire all his pupils to learn to the maximum of their ability. He is not only interested in conveying facts and figures, but also to endow in his pupils understanding, to develop in them a questioning mind, and to awaken the thrill of discovery with which all children are born, but often lose before they progress very far in many schools.

Principals of schools, who are responsible for evaluating the teachers on the staff, will tell you that it's fairly easy to identify the superior teacher and the poor teacher. It's those in the middle, who need help in some phases of their teaching, who are most resistant to criticism and assistance.

What does a principal look for when he observes a teacher in action? How does he judge her competency? He looks for:

Motivation. He wants to see *all* the children in the room participating. If some child is inattentive, he expects to see the teacher take steps to draw that child into the mainstream of the lesson. However, in all fairness, it must be pointed out that this is not always possible for the teacher to accomplish at that particular moment, but the principal, in discussing the lesson with the teacher later, would want to know what follow-up action the teacher planned to take, particularly if the action of the child was consistently inattentive. Had the teacher talked to the child? Had the teacher used incentives to bring out the curiosity and interests of the child? Had she consulted with the guidance counsellor? With the parent? Had the child been seen recently by a medical doctor to make sure there was no physical cause for the lack of attention? Had some catastrophic event happened in the child's life? A superior teacher is constantly aware of each child's attitude, behavior, and physical condition.

Enthusiasm. Some teachers are fortunate to be born with the ability to inspire others through the enthusiasm that they exude. Their eyes sparkle. Their voices reflect the excitement they feel about the subject they are teaching. They move about the classroom; they single out individual pupils who are losing interest or whose attention is temporarily diverted to something closer at hand, and they talk directly to them, hoping to draw them back into the mainstream. They are constantly at the blackboard making sketches, jotting down important points; examining the work of individual students to ascertain if they are doing prescribed written work, helping those who are having difficulty, pointing out errors, encouraging any who seem to be losing interest.

On the other hand, you have the teacher who sits at his desk, talks in a monotone, appears to be bored by his own voice, seldom goes to the blackboard to emphasize some point he is trying to make, and assigns mountains of "desk work," so he can sit behind his desk and perhaps doze off occasionally.

Enthusiasm in a teacher is most critical in the lower grades but becomes less important in the upper grades. However, this does not infer that the enthusiastic teacher is any less desirable in the middle and high school; it implies that a student is more forgiving as he advances through the grades and is more tolerant of a teacher who acts with moderation and restraint. Also in all fairness, there are many teachers who are not overly exuberant, yet do inspire their students and turn out well-informed, educated students.

Clarity. A teacher who lacks clarity leaves his pupils confused, frustrated and—eventually—unmotivated. A teacher at all grade levels, must be able to express himself clearly, logically and, at the same time, succinctly. Here is a partial list of the types of explanations and directions a typical teacher at all grade levels must perform during a typical school day:

1. How pupils are to line up to go to the boys' and girls' rooms.
2. How each student is to prepare his written work including: information to be contained in the heading of his papers, format, indentations, margin widths, use of cursive or printed letters, kinds of paper which are acceptable, pencil or pen, neatness criteria, etc.
3. How papers are to be passed in.
4. In detail, what the homework assignment is, how it is to be prepared, and when it is due.
5. Assigning reading groups, designating where they are to assemble, what they are to do until the teacher comes to their group to work with them, and what workbooks or readers they are to work from.
6. How the class is to go to the assembly, where they are to sit, and how they are to behave.
7. Instructions for a fire drill.
8. Explanations for each written lesson: pages covered, questions to be answered, type of answer (should they be in complete sentences? essay type? in ink? in pencil?).

This list could go on and on. A teacher's day consists of one set of directions after another, some simple, some complex. And to be successful, *every* pupil must hear and understand the directions. Not that easy! "Does everyone understand what I just said?" the teacher will ask. No one indicates otherwise. "Are you all sure?" she repeats. Again, everyone indicates that he does.

Ten minutes later, when 95 percent of the class is busily engaged in following through with the directions, there's little Johnnie and Mary in the back of the room staring off into space, pencils idle, books closed. The problem was that they weren't paying attention when the directions were given *and* they weren't paying attention when the teacher asked the class if they understood the directions!

Even more important than giving clear directions is presenting a lesson so that even the pupil with the lowest I.Q. in the class can understand it. This, too, is not an easy task. To make subject matter clear to a pupil with an I.Q. of 85 or 90, the teacher will undoubtedly have to repeat the material several times. However, repetition of the same material in the same way can easily cause a student with an I.Q. of 120 or higher to become impatient and bored, with the result that he loses interest and turns his attention to something else. The gifted teacher will attempt to make the second explanation different, approaching it from another angle, making use of audiovisual material, graphs, maps, blackboard, or demonstrations.

Making the Material Interesting. A principal expects the superior teacher to make his material so interesting that his pupils are disappointed when the class comes to an end. The secret of such success lies in the use of a wide variety of teaching techniques—described below:

Games:	The teacher must be familiar with at least a dozen games, each with a different objective. Most of these games should include everyone in the class and should usually contain plenty of action.
Playacting:	A useful technique when the teacher is attempting to teach the class some moral principle or to promote an attitudinal or behavioral concept. Each student is assigned a role and is encouraged to ad lib, with some direction from the teacher as to how the action should progress. A predicament, common to the age of the child is then presented to the group, and they are asked to respond with a solution.
Story Telling:	This can be done either by reading from a book or told from the teacher's repertoire.
Play periods:	Every nursery school or kindergarten room should be furnished with many different types of educational toys, games, and apparatus. During these periods of supervised play, the teacher is interested not only in noting the competency of the child in mastering the particular toy or game he has chosen, but also in observing the interaction of the children one with another.
Child Response:	This type of activity is one in which each child is given the opportunity to tell the rest of the class about some personal experience he has had.
Other Activities:	May include: parties; guests from the community, such as librarians, policemen, crossing guards; visits to the firehouse, post office, etc.; singing and singing games; rest periods; and occasional use of television, movies or the phonograph.

Before leaving the subject of teacher competency, some discussion of tenure is in order. In most states a teacher obtains tenure after serving a school district for three years. Once tenure is obtained, that teacher cannot be fired except for gross incompetency or conviction of a crime. To prove gross incompetency is usually a difficult task. Local, state, and national teachers organizations immediately come to the defense of the teacher. The case is usually so long drawn-out and so costly that most boards of education are adverse to becoming involved. As a result, our nation's schoolrooms are filled with great numbers of incompetent teachers.

In Norfolk, Ohio, the board of education attempted to fire a tenured teacher on the grounds that she could not maintain discipline in her classroom or on the school grounds during recess. The teachers' union took the case to court, and after a lengthy and costly trial won the case, because the Board had failed to prove that the teacher was *grossly* inefficient.

As a result of the difficulty and expense involved in dismissal of tenured teachers, boards of education have virtually given up any attempt to rid their districts of inferior teachers; instead, they await the teacher's retirement, or, in extreme cases, may transfer the teacher to a nonteaching position at the same salary.

How did tenure come about? To some extent, the boards of education of the early twentieth century were to blame. During that period, the practice of hiring a teacher for a few years and then dismissing her became a common practice. The reasoning behind this was that a board of education could save the taxpayers (themselves included) a great deal of money by having low-paying, beginning teachers on their staff. The practice became so notorious that the growing teachers' unions of the day (the NEA and its state affiliates) pressured the state legislatures to pass protective measures for their teachers. As a result, tenure laws were finally enacted in all fifty states.

It is time that these tenure laws were modified to make it easier for a board of education to rid itself of unfit faculty members. Until that happens, the government and the people must understand that part of the problem affecting our schools is because of these tenure statutes.

An example of how these tenure laws are holding back improvement in our schools is exemplified by a case in the New York City schools. A Bronx elementary principal was arrested on drug charges; before this arrest he had been suspended three separate times for "poor leadership" and such other problems as failure to report for work. Parents had also complained about Matthew Barnwell's sloppy appearance and his failure to exert leadership in his school. Several years earlier he had been temporarily transferred to an office job because of his inefficiency. Board member Jerome Greene had hoped the transfer could be made permanent, but Barnwell made the threat that he would go through a formal grievance procedure. The teachers' union also entered the picture, and the board gave in. Then Barnwell was arrested on the drug charges. He was caught buying two vials of crack in Manhattan.

In Chicago, where 28,000 certified employees are on staff, only seven discharges of certified personnel were brought to a hearing by the Chicago Board of Education. Each case cost the taxpayers about $30,000.

Another set of laws which hamper school administrators from ridding their faculty of poor teachers are the so-called seniority laws. These laws detail in great depth how a school district will cut back the number of teachers on its staff when declining enrollments dictate this action. Ah, you say, here's an excellent opportunity to remove all the dead wood! Not so, unfortunately. Teachers must be let go according to when they were hired—the most recent first.

In most school districts the most recently hired are usually the better teachers because administrators, now very much aware of what tenure can do to their faculty, spend considerable time with these teachers, working with them, evaluating them, and letting the incompetent go by the third year.

3. **Discipline.** Discipline has been defined as "the type of climate required in a classroom for maximum learning to take place." It may vary from situation to situation. Examples: A teacher proctoring a written examination by a group of students would be expected to maintain absolute silence in the room. No student would be permitted to be in a posture which would enable him to see what was on another student's paper. On the other hand, a teacher supervising a physical education class would be primarily concerned with conducting the game in progress according to the rules, seeing that all students participated, and making sure that nothing took place which could threaten the safety of any student.

It's not always easy for an administrator who is evaluating a class to determine whether the teacher is maintaining the degree of discipline necessary for optimum learning to take place. Let's look at a few examples.

When the administrator enters this fifth grade class, the teacher is conducting a discussion of why the pilgrims decided to leave their homeland and sail to the New World. The discussion is moved forward by a series of questions from the teacher. Several children feverishly wave their hands about over their heads. Several, in their excitement, shout out answers. The teacher welcomes these answers and makes no attempt to hold the children back by requiring them to raise their hands and be called upon for an answer.

Is this atmosphere conducive to good learning? In some ways, yes. To require hands to be raised and individuals called upon for answers might stifle the enthusiasm. On the other hand, only the very aggressive students are being heard. The timid ones soon learn to lower their hands and "take a back seat" to what is going on. Some may even withdraw from the class and find something else to occupy their thoughts.

Probably the way the teacher should handle this is to permit the more aggressive students to have their way for a while, and then put a halt to their monopolizing the lesson by informing the class that now hands must be raised. The teacher would then make a point of calling on some of the quieter, less aggressive students.

Now supposing that when the administrator entered this class he found that two boys in the back of the room had moved their desks together and were playing some kind of game and only occasionally looking up to see what was going on in the front of the room. A girl had her head down on the desk and was apparently either sick or sleeping. Two other boys were leaning over the aisle between their desks and were whispering to each other. An paper airplane sailed across the room, but the teacher was looking the other way and didn't see it. A girl had earphones on and a small radio hidden in her desk.

In this situation it is evident that the teacher is beginning to lose control of her class.

The final stage in complete loss of control will come when none of the students in the room are listening to the teacher, when she is screaming for them to keep quiet, when students are out of their seats and moving about the room, throwing spitballs, when the boys are hitting the girls over the head with books, when radios are playing, when pupils leave the room without permission or lean out the window to yell at someone outside, when the floor is littered with papers and trash, and when the pupils have no fear of shouting insults at the teacher or making snide remarks to her. And the louder she screams at them to be quiet, the more fun they have taunting her.

When classroom discipline has sunk to this level, there is no way that it can ever be restored. Even if she is moved to another class, word spreads among pupils, and she will face the same problem there. Occasionally, moving such a teacher to another school building in the district will work—*if* that teacher has profited by her mistakes.

Let's look at another example. A first-grade teacher is conducting a reading session. She has divided the class of twenty-six pupils into three reading groups: slow, medium, and fast, named Bluebirds, Robins, and Canaries. At the time the principal enters the room to make an evaluation, she is working with the Bluebirds. The Robins and Canaries are working at their seats on an assignment in their reading workbooks.

The Bluebirds are gathered in a circle in another part of the room with the teacher. She is listening to each of the nine pupils as he reads. She helps Tommy when he has trouble pronouncing a word. She illustrates several rules of phonics on the blackboard behind her so Sally can understand why a particular word is pronounced as it is.

The teacher is also cognizant of what the rest of her class is doing. Occasionally she may address one of them. She may tell Susy that she's not paying enough attention to her work, or reprimand John because he's talking to his neighbor.

Any of these students at their seat know that if he has a problem he may raise his hand and get permission to come to the teacher for help. She will interrupt her reading group long enough to help that child.

After about twenty minutes the teacher will take another reading group. However, she will give more time to the Bluebirds because they are the poorest of her readers and need the most help.

The principal should be pleased when he leaves this room. This is an experienced teacher who has conducted a lesson she can be proud of.

Evaluation

Place an x for each entry to rate your child's school. Then connect the x's with a continuous line to form a graph. 1 = low; 5 = high

1 2 3 4 5

- Teacher-classroom ratio, Kindergarten (Maximum: 1 to 20).
- Teacher-classroom ratio, Grades 1 through 6 (Maximum: 1 to 25).
- Number of teachers without a degree (There should be none).
- Percent of teachers with a BA degree (No more than 60%).
- Percent of teachers with a MA degree (The higher percentage, the higher the evaluation).
- Your child's teacher demonstrates that she has an excellent command of written English.

- Your child's teacher demonstrates superior knowledge of the subjects taught.
- Your child's teacher motivates *all* pupils to do their best.
- Your child's teacher uses a wide variety of teaching *techniques*.
- Your child's teacher uses a wide variety of teaching *aids*.
- Your child's teacher gives clear, concise directions.
- Your child's teacher is successful in making lessons clear to *all* pupils.
- Pupils in your child's class go about their classroom routines with a minimum of confusion.
- Your child's teacher makes her lessons interesting.
- The Board of Education has taken steps to rid its schools of poor teachers.
- Rate your teacher on classroom control.

If possible, enlist as many neighbors and friends who have pupils in the school to complete the above evaluation for as many teachers in different grades as possible. By doing this you will obtain a broader picture of the school's complete staff.

MEDIA SPECIALIST (LIBRARIAN)

Every parent should spend at least several hours visiting the school's media center. Gone are the days when an elementary school's "library" consisted of a few shelves of books in each classroom, or, at best, a roving wagon that visited all the classrooms once a day and allowed pupils to select books.

Today's media center is centrally located in the school and contains at least three or four square feet of space for each student enrolled in the school. In addition the center should contain the following features: (1) an office for the media specialist; (2) a preparation room where books can be catalogued, films edited, periodicals processed and library reference works shelved; (3) a room for filing back issues of magazines, newspapers, and other periodicals; (4) a room for storage of tapes, records, films, film strips, movies, etc. This room may be in combination with number 3.

For further information about the physical layout of the media center, refer to Chapter Two, Physical Plant.

The media specialist should have at least a master's degree in her field. She should have apprenticed for a minimum of one year and then should have an additional year or two as an assistant.

The media specialist initiates and puts into practice the activities that take place within the media center. There are a number of ways the observer can determine how effectively the media specialist, through her subordinates, is providing a rich environment for the pupils of the school. The following should be looked at:

1. *Displays.* There should be sections of the room or bulletin boards set apart for promoting, through displays, recommended books to be read, new films that have been purchased, travelogues, topics of interest, special displays for teachers who are emphasizing certain areas of their subject matter, or latest news bulletins. If at all possible, it should be ascertained as to how often these displays are changed; in some schools such displays have been around for several years!

2. *Book Purchases.* Spend time going through the stacks, asking such questions as: What percentage of these books are copyrighted within the past few years? How many of them look as if they had been purchased at a secondhand book store or left over from some fire sale? What percentage of the books are being used by the students? (Look in the back and check through the date stamps to see how long an interval exists between each withdrawal.) Are all topics covered by an adequate number of books? Are the books within each category different from one another in their approach and coverage? Are the books arranged by the Dewey Decimal System or some other accepted method of classification? Are the books being kept in good repair? Are the books being returned to their proper position on the shelves? What method is used to return them (volunteer students, volunteer parents, paid assistants)? Are some volumes covered with dust, indicating they are never read, indicating that they should be permanently removed from the shelves? How many nonfiction books does the center contain? How many fiction? (In a school, the nonfiction should outweigh the fiction by at least three to one.) Are the fiction titles in line with the moral and ethical standards of the community? On the other hand, is there any indication that personal bias has kept worthwhile books off the shelves?

3. *Student Use.* The main criteria of how effective a school's media center is can be determined by observing student activity throughout a typical day.

What to Look For. Before actually observing the activities of the students using the media center, count the seating capacity of the room. Ten percent of the student body is a fair judge of the minimum number of seats that should be available. For an elementary school of five hundred, therefore, fifty seats would be minimal.

Library seating is usually provided in the form of comfortable chairs situated around a table. As students enter, it will be observed that they usually come in pairs or groups and tend to occupy the same table, usually crowding together at one end. As they enter at the beginning of the period make note of the following: How quickly they get down to work; Whether they use the library facilities or do work that could just as easily be done in a study hall. Converse among themselves to the point where it is obvious they are not making the best use of their time. Are they supervised by an adult member of the media staff. Do they have easy access to the card catalog (or the computer terminal if the library has been modernized). Make use of many facets of the center (books, periodicals, slide projectors, tapes, film strips, etc.), which indicates that they have been given an orientation course in media use. Take care of library material.

Don't be afraid to ask questions of students and media personnel. Of course, it should be done tactfully. Some of the questions that might be asked of students: How much of your homework requires the use of the media center? How much of your classroom work? Does your teacher ever make assignments which require the entire class to visit the media center? If so, does the teacher prepare the class ahead of time as to where the assignment can be found? Some questions which might be asked of the media personnel: Is the media center closed to other students when a class is using the center? How much money is budgeted each year for replacement and for new media software?

Evaluation

Rate each of the following statements by placing an x beneath the letter that best describes the conditions in your community's schools. Then connect the x's with a continuous line to form a graph.

1   2   3   4   5

- The media center is centrally located.
- The media center contains:
    An office for the media specialists
    A preparation room
    A room for the storage of periodicals, tapes, etc.
    A periodical storage room.
- The media center contains interesting displays.
- The media center contains a comprehensive collection of fiction and nonfiction books.

- The media center contains a comprehensive collection of tapes, records, film strips. etc.
- The media center contains sufficient seating capacity.
- The student body makes good use of all features of the media center.
- The pupils using the media center are supervised.
- Teachers make assignments which require the use of the media center.
- Teachers bring their entire class to the media center.
- Pupils have been indoctrinated in the use of all areas of the media center.

TEACHERS OF ATYPICAL PUPILS

Not all children are born with equal mental ability; the range runs from the idiot through the genius. Others are handicapped—blind, hard of hearing, physically impaired. When a pupil's handicap is so severe that he has difficulty competing with other children his age, he is removed from the mainstream and placed in a special class. He is referred to as an atypical pupil.

Teachers for these atypical pupils are highly trained in their field. In most states, at least a master's degree is required in order to receive certification. Special equipment may be necessary in order to best serve these pupils. Teacher-pupil ratios are small.

The latest thinking regarding the education of the atypical pupil is that he should be removed from the mainstream as little as is necessary. This is accomplished by scheduling the pupil in such a way that he visits his special teacher during those times when his regular class is at art, music, physical education, or recess. The amount of time he is away is determined by how severe his handicap is.

In evaluating your school to determine its effectiveness in taking care of the needs of the atypical pupil, the lay person is not qualified to go into great depth. Use the following evaluation as a guideline.

Evaluation

Rate each of the following statements by placing an x beneath the appropriate number. Then connect the x's with a continuous line to form a graph.

                                                    1 2 3 4 5

- The school system has provided for the education of all atypical pupils.
- Teachers for these classes are adequately trained and properly certified.
- Teacher-pupil ratios are low enough so that individual instruction is possible.
- Specialized equipment is provided.
- Pupils are mainstreamed as much as possible.

PHYSICAL EDUCATION TEACHERS

In the lower grades, kindergarten through two or three, physical education is usually conducted by the classroom teacher in the form of playground recess. However, in some schools, the physical education teacher may give some of his time, in conjunction with the classroom teacher, to instruct these pupils in the rudiments of the type of games and activities they will be performing as they advance through the grades. Volleyball, soccer, touch football may be added to the simpler type of games these children have experienced during their playground activities (tag, hide-and-go-seek, maypole, dodge ball, etc.).

As is obvious, a physical education teacher's training does not have to be as proficient in the academics as a classroom teacher's. Instead, he must be familiar with a host of physical activities and games. He must have a personality that not only brings him respect but one that is also compassionate and understanding. He must realize and take into consideration that not all his pupils have the same interests and abilities in the area of sports.

The masculine gender has been used in the above only because it would be awkward to continually refer to both sexes. However, there are, in the public schools, an equal number of female physical education teachers, and one of the requisites of a good physical education department is that there are at least an equal number of male and female teachers.

Before examining the qualities of a good physical education teacher, it should be noted that the number of times a class is scheduled each week is important. Five times a week for forty-five minutes each day is better than three times a week for an hour and a half. Pupils need a daily break in their studies; they also need exercise each day.

Let's examine the duties of a physical education teacher in the upper grades of an elementary school. When does the physical education teacher's duties begin? Not when the boys and girls enter the gymnasium dressed in their gym outfits. It begins when the boys enter the locker room to change their clothes. (Usually a female gym teacher is scheduled with a another class at the same time as the male gym teacher; the male teacher supervises the boys' locker room for both classes, and the female teacher does the same for the girls.)

After roll call most physical education teachers lead the class in calisthenics to make sure that all the pupils are properly "warmed up" before beginning any competitive sports. Following calisthenics the teacher will then inform the class about what game or activity will be played for the remainder of the period. Before commencing the game, the teacher should take some time to review the rules and perhaps show the class certain maneuvers or plays which will help the pupils play the game better.

A conscientious physical education teacher will enter into the sport along with the rest of the class, or he may officiate, or he may stand off at the sidelines and make sure that the game goes according to accepted practices. Occasionally he may interrupt the game to show a player how he could have made a better play, or to instruct the entire class in some fundamental principle of the game. At the end of the period he accompanies the boys into the shower room and supervises while they shower and dress.

During the class he will make observations concerning the performance of each pupil. He may do this by placing a grade in his marking book, or make a comment in a ledger he keeps so that during the next class he can take the child aside and help him improve his game. He will make note of those boys and girls who are not dressed properly for gym, and he will also make note of those who do not take showers, passing this information on to the female physical education teacher for her pupils.

Then there is the physical education teacher at the other end of the scale. More than likely he will toss in the ball, get the game started, and then go off to talk to the janitor, catch a smoke in the teachers' room, or grab an early lunch. And more than one of this type of teacher has found himself in court because an accident occurred while he was away from his group.

A good physical education teacher should have the following qualities: a pleasant, friendly relationship with his pupils, a thorough knowledge of all games suited to the grade levels he teaches, ability to communicate and explain, a love and respect of children, ability to gain the respect and admiration of his pupils, fairness, and the understanding and knowledge that not all children have the same athletic ability.

He should also be adequately trained to take care of the needs of those children who are physically handicapped, mentally handicapped, overweight, hard of hearing, visually impaired, and emotionally disturbed.

Evaluation

Rate the following statements by placing an x beneath the appropriate number. Then connect the x's with a continuous line to form a graph.

                                                                1   2   3   4   5

- Your child's school employs an equal number of male and female teachers.
- Your child receives P.E. every day of the week.
- Your child's teacher supervises the class while pupils are dressing.
- Your child's teacher conducts some type of warmup exercises.
- Your child's teacher takes attendance to make sure no one is missing.
- Your child's teacher supervises all activities for the entire class period.
- Your child's teacher instructs through explanations and demonstrations.
- Your child's teacher seems to have the admiration and respect of his class.
- Your child's teacher takes notes or marks pupil performance during class.

SCHOOL NURSE

The school nurse should have a degree in school nursing and should be certified by the state. Most of all, she should like to work with children, understand their problems, and be ready to counsel them in matters of health, personal hygiene, and if necessary, to help them solve personal problems which might be brought to her attention.

Needless to say, she should be proficient in all first aid requirements and able to diagnose simple diseases. She should know when an injury or ailment is serious enough to require a doctor's immediate care, or when an ambulance is needed.

She should keep adequate health records of each pupil, make routine examinations, usually under the supervision of the school's physician and dentist, and from time to time, examine the faculty according to the regulations of the state in which the school is situated.

The nurse's "suite" should contain a rest room where sick children can lie down until their parents arrive to pick them up. There should also be an examination room, toilets, and possibly a separate room to serve as an office.

Evaluation

Rate the following statements by placing an x beneath the appropriate number. Then connect the x's with a continuous line to form a graph.

                                                           1   2   3   4   5

- The school nurse has at least a BA degree in school nursing.
- The school nurse demonstrates a proficiency in taking care of pupils' health needs.
- The school nurse demonstrates the ability to handle an emergency or crisis.
- The school nurse keeps adequate health records for the pupils and faculty.
- The nurse's suite contains sufficient space and equipment for the size of the school.

GUIDANCE

Until recently guidance counsellors were considered necessary only in the secondary schools where, originally, their sole purpose was to guide students into taking the necessary courses to obtain admission to the best colleges.

The role of the guidance counsellor in the elementary school has grown since its introduction in the late 1960s when counsellors from the high school would, for a week or two each year, venture down to the upper elementary grades to help students select their courses of study for their high school years.

At first, the counsellors in the elementary schools were part-time positions; in larger districts a high school counsellor would be assigned part time to one of the elementary schools. As time went on, however, the need for full-time counsellors became apparent.

The classroom teachers were the first to express this need. There were times when pupils in their classes presented emotional problems which they were not equipped to handle. The inner cities felt this need first, but as time went on, the problem spread to the suburbs and the country.

As drug addiction became an elementary school problem as well as a high school problem, the role of the guidance counsellor broadened.

In today's school the guidance department handles a broad spectrum of problems, the extent of which is usually described in the district's job description manual. Certain problems may be assigned to the principal or vice principal, or may be designated to the guidance department.

The following is a partial list of these duties:

Chronic absenteeism
Alcoholism
Drug abuse
Apparent parental neglect or abuse
Emotional problems
Severe behavioral problems
Repetitive sleeping in class
Sex-related problems
Poor grades
Tardiness
Liaison between school and parents/guardians
Record-keeping
Periodic pupil interviews initiated by the guidance department
Referral to the nurse for apparent uncleanliness, nits, scalp conditions, disease, etc.
Referrals to the school psychologist when considered necessary

Counselling in the elementary school requires a special kind of person. Qualities which make for an outstanding guidance counsellor:

1. The ability to listen and give counsel without passing judgment.
2. Understanding and empathy for the problems of elementary school-aged children.
3. In-depth knowledge of child and adolescent psychology.
4. The ability to converse at the child's level.
5. An innate gift of being able to fathom the thoughts and feelings of others.
6. In-touch experience with the life styles of the pupils in the school.
7. An optimistic outlook on life.
8. A well-rounded, adjusted personal life.
9. Ability to keep detailed, meaningful records.

In most states a master's degree is required for certification as a guidance counsellor; many have doctorates.

Evaluation

Rate the following statements by placing an x beneath the appropriate number. Then connect the x's with a continuous line to form a graph.

1 2 3 4 5

- Your child's school has a guidance department.
- The ratio of counsellors to pupils is at least 1 to 200.
- All counsellors have a master's degree or better.
- A special "suite" of offices is provided for the guidance department.
- Each counsellor has a private, soundproof office.
- Your child meets with his guidance counsellor at least twice a year, exclusive of pupil requested meetings.
- Rate your child's counsellor on each of the following: (Numbers refer to the qualities listed in the above text.)

  1.
  2.
  3.
  4.
  5.
  6.
  7.
  8.
  9.

CLERKS AND SECRETARIES

Although not a part of the professional staff of a school, the clerks and secretaries play an important role. It's the front-desk clerk or secretary who first greets visitors, and the impression she makes often carries over to any subsequent encounters with other members of the staff.

A large elementary school will probably have about five clerks and secretaries: Secretary to the principal, perhaps shared by the vice-principal(s). Secretary to the guidance department, often shared by the nurse. Clerks who are skilled in taking and recording attendance, usually done by a computer. A "front desk" clerk, who greets visitors, takes incoming telephone calls, manages the switchboard, and perhaps arranges for substitute teachers.

Evaluation

Rate the following statements by placing an x beneath the appropriate number. Then connect the x's with a continuous line to form a graph.

1   2   3   4   5

- Your child's school has an adequate number of secretaries and clerks.
- The secretaries and clerks show proficiency in their assigned tasks.

Chapter Seven

SECONDARY SCHOOL STAFF

The curriculum of a secondary school is only as effective as the ability of its teaching staff to breathe life into it. A well-developed course of study can be ineffective in the hands of an inferior teacher, and a mediocre curriculum can be brought to fruition by a creative teacher. The course of study serves only as a guide; the teacher must build upon it and give it life.

Courses of study which have been developed mainly by the teachers who will later use them will have a far greater chance of success than those written by a department head or a group of outside "experts" who have been hired by the board of education. (Such an "expert" might be defined as a mediocre consultant who comes from a distance at a high salary to perform a task that could better be done by the local staff.)

The secondary school is a highly complex organization; its success depends entirely upon the staff of teachers, specialists, administrators, and lay personnel who plan its curriculum, devise and enforce its rules and regulations, and instruct its students. It is not static. It varies in its effectiveness from year to year and within each school year.

This chapter will focus on the staff of teachers and specialists who make up the modern high school. The following topics will be examined:

(1) How high school teachers differ from their counterparts in the elementary school.

(2) Duties and responsibilities of a high school teacher outside the classroom.

(3) Good and bad personality traits of teachers which are common to all high school teaching staffs.

(4) Typical parental complaints about teachers.

(5) Two personnel sketches to illustrate the effective and the noneffective high school teacher.

How High School Teachers Differ from their Counterparts in the Elementary School

As has been pointed out in Chapter Six, the basic responsibility of the elementary teacher is to turn out students who have mastered the fundamentals and who have acquired good study habits. Teaching the basics requires that a teacher be informed in a number of subjects—reading, writing, arithmetic, science, and social studies, and possessing the capability to lead the class in singing and games. An elementary school teacher's knowledge is broad but superficial.

On the other hand, the high school teacher has in-depth knowledge in one or two subjects. From the first day he entered a teacher-training institution, his studies focused, for the most part, on his major and minor fields.

The elementary school teacher is trained in early childhood psychology. Dealing with children from five years of age to the early teens requires a technique far different from that of the secondary school teacher. Patience and understanding are essential.

Because repetition is a necessary teaching technique, the elementary school teacher must have those personal qualities which will prevent him from "burnout" due to boredom and ennui. Dealing with small children, day after day, has an accumulative effect on certain types of individuals. One first-grade elementary school teacher with whom I was talking recently told me, "Sometimes when I get home at night I find myself talking and thinking like a six-year-old. And when I'm with adults again it takes me a while to get acclimated."

Teaching teen-agers, who are closer in mental, social, and physical age to the instructor, is far more satisfying intellectually. However, it takes a special kind of person to be able to get along with teen-agers, and unfortunately, there are too few of them in our high schools.

Duties and Responsibilities of the High School Teacher Outside the Classroom

The largest percent of high schools schedule seven periods each day. Of these seven periods, five are regular class periods (except for language arts teachers, who, in many schools are assigned only four periods to give them added time for the correction of essays and compositions), one is a so-called "free" period or "preparation period," and the seventh is reserved for special assignments.

Following is a list of some of the more typical of these assignments. Not all of them fall within one of the regular seven periods of the day, and in that case the teacher is given compensatory time to make up for the loss of a lunch period or other time which is normally unassigned.

1. *Supervision of a Study Hall.* Many high schools, it is true, have done away with study halls. However, there are still a number of schools who find them profitable or who must include them to act as a "free agent" while scheduling classes, particularly when the computer rejects a large percentage of student schedules which must then be done by hand.

The tendency of many schools is to place study halls in the cafeteria or auditorium or any other large room in order to free regular classrooms for class work. Supervision in these large rooms is difficult and teachers are reluctant to have them assigned to them. In a large room at least two teachers must be assigned or discipline is likely to break down.

2. *Hall Supervision.* One problem facing high schools is the student who is constantly roaming the halls, peering into his friend's classroom, meeting other students at a prearranged time, or staying for long periods of time in the boys' or girls' room to smoke a cigarette or a reefer.

All schools, therefore, require that each student who is in the hallway while classes are in session be in possession of a "hall pass." This pass will give the time the student left his assigned room, the number of the classroom, the destination of the student and the teacher's signature.

The teacher(s) assigned to hall patrol are required to check each student to make sure he has a valid pass.

Some schools have used honor students instead of teachers to monitor the hallways with some success. The results depend entirely on the make-up of the student body. In inner city schools the system would probably never work (often police are hired for this purpose), but in some suburban and country schools, I have seen it administered with good results. This is particularly true in schools where the system has been in use for many years and has become a tradition.

3. *Clubs and Other Extracurricular Activities.* The modern high school encourages the formation of many different kinds of clubs. Often each teacher is responsible for sponsoring a club, and a special period is entered into the daily schedule for meetings to take place. This is accomplished by taking five or ten minutes off each regular period.

The types of clubs and other activities in high schools across the country is limitless, but a few of the more common ones would include:

Chess Club	Future Nurses
Dramatics Club	Future Housewives
School Newspaper	Science Club
School Magazine	Debating Club
Key Club (Kiwanis)	Foreign Language Club
Nature Club	Home Economics Club
Astronomy Club	Future Pilots
Sports Club	Historical Society
Honor Society	Art Club
Literary Club	Glee Club
Library Helpers	Auto Repair Club
Future Teachers of America	Bird Watchers

4. *Lunchroom-Cafeteria Supervision.* At least two teachers are assigned to each lunch hour. Their duties include: (1) preventing students from infiltrating into the rest of the building (two-thirds of the student body will be in class and movement in the hallways can be distracting to teachers and students), (2) keeping the noise level low enough so that eating can be a pleasure, (3) making sure students throw their waste in the slop pails and not at each other, (4) keeping students in their seats after they have finished eating, (5) preventing fights, (6) conducting an orderly and safe disbursement of the students into the hallways at the bell indicating the end of that lunch period.

5. *Fire Drills.* While fire drills are conducted during regular school time when classes are in session, most teachers consider it an extra duty. Keeping hundreds of teenagers in line, keeping them quiet enough so they could hear any orders that might be necessary, is a momentous task and one that the staff does not enjoy.

6. *Committee Meetings.* A modern high school probably could not exist for very long were it not for teachers' meetings. The principal will usually conduct a meeting at least once a month to discuss problems that need teacher-input before they can be solved.

Department heads meet regularly with the teachers in their department to work on curricula, to assist in making textbook selections, to gather budget information for the following school year, or to solve any problems within the department.

In addition there are usually a number of ad hoc committees in existence throughout the year whose duty it is to come up with recommendations for consideration by the entire faculty. Such topics as revision of the marking system, report card format changes, what to do for American Education Week, how to curtail students from going across the street to the mall during lunch hour, or how to prevent students from cutting assembly are all typical topics for these ad hoc committees.

Often representative students and parents are invited to take part in the discussions that go on during the meetings of the ad hoc committees.

7. *Curriculum Revision.* Curriculum revision usually takes place within each department. But there is also needed a liaison between departments to coordinate the curricula and to make sure there is no duplication.

8. *Bus Loading and Unloading.* The number of high schools where students do not arrive by bus are few and far between, confined mostly to the large city districts. And even here, with the advent of the Supreme Court's ruling to bring racial balance to the schools, busing students from white neighborhoods to black schools and vice versa has become a common practice.

To insure the safety of students and to ward off possible lawsuits against the district, most schools require that a certified member of the staff be on duty when buses arrive in the morning and when students board them again after school for the return trip.

9. *Locker Inspections.* School officials have limited access to students' lockers after several court decisions nixed searching at random without just cause. However, if prior notice of sufficient time is given, teachers may examine the lockers of the students in their home room to make sure that the accumulations of old papers and other debris does not pose a fire hazard.

The idea behind giving prior notice is to motivate the students to clean out their lockers before the inspection takes place.

10. *Assembly Presentations.* Many schools have abandoned most assemblies because student control is difficult. However, for those who still maintain this time-honored custom, student-produced plays, skits, amateur shows, and musical presentations make for a relaxing break in the school day. Homeroom teachers and special subject teachers are encouraged to put on these productions, and, in some schools, it is a required function.

11. *Chaperone Dances and Other Afternoon and Evening Events.* Each year the graduating classes of the nation's schools sponsor a senior prom, and senior class advisors are the chaperones. Other evening functions requiring the presence of the staff are P.T.A. meetings, Back to School Night, dramatic productions, fashion shows, and various athletic events.

The local chapter of the National Education Association in most schools across the country, in their bargaining sessions with the boards of education, have won extra compensation for attendance at any event which occurs after school hours.

Good and Bad Personality Traits of Teachers Common to All High School Teaching Staffs

A high school with an enrollment of between a thousand and two thousand students will have a staff of teachers, specialists, and lay personnel of from 80 to 150. It is only natural with this many individuals that all types of personalities will be represented, some with annoying habits and character traits which drive the administrators to drink, and others who go out of their way to help out whenever they are needed. In most cases none of these traits are sufficient enough in themselves to warrant dismissal proceedings to be initiated. However, the administration will certainly hold counsel with each individual in an attempt to remedy the problem. Some of the more prevalent complaints could be summed up briefly thus:

The Griper. This is the guy or gal who spends most of his time in the teachers' room finding fault with his students, his schedule, the food in the cafeteria, his parking spot, the condition of the roadway into the school—you name it, he's complained about it at some time or another to his fellow teachers (Never to the administration!). And he's the fellow who's too busy to volunteer when a committee is formed to find solutions to any one of the problems he's been griping about.

The Teacher Who's on His Way to His Car When the Faculty Dismissal Bell Rings. He's the last one to arrive at school in the morning, too—and the first in lunch line. An administrator can only wonder why this man continues to teach—anyone who cuts his day so short cannot possibly be happy in his work.

The Teacher Who's Habitually Absent and Late. In most states the law awards a teacher one day a month for absenteeism. Some school districts add to this—a few days for "personal business," days for death in the family, and time for women faculty members who have to remain home to take care of young children who are sick.

Every school system has the teacher who has exhausted all of his allowable sick days and is now being docked for every day he is absent. Sometimes his absences are unavoidable because of prolonged illnesses. But often this type of individual stays at home because he doesn't feel like getting up in the morning, or because he dreads facing his classes for another day, or because he has a drinking problem.

This kind of teacher has no scruples whatsoever in approaching the board of education at one of its meetings to ask for additional paid leave of absence.

Administrators wonder why it is that some of their teachers go year after year with hardly an absence, and others are totally delinquent in their attendance. One administrator kept a list of the reasons offered by one of his teachers who was absent at least once each week: "I had a headache. I couldn't sleep all night. I had to go shopping. My sister is visiting me. My mother in Chicago needed me. My car wouldn't start. My furnace went on the blink and I had to stay home so the repairman could get into the house."

Although this teacher is now being docked for his absences, nevertheless the money the board of education saves does not compensate for the lack of continuity in the teaching that his students are subjected to. Even the best of substitute teachers cannot expect to teach with the same proficiency as that of the regular teacher. Usually the substitute teacher is forced to give his classes "busy work" because he does not wish to proceed with new work which he might present in a way contrary to the wishes of the regular teacher.

The Bragger. Every school has at least one of these. His favorite milieu is the teachers' meeting. He's the guy who interrupts another teacher who is in the process of describing a teaching technique that's been used with some success. He interrupts because he has a much better technique, and he proceeds to elucidate in glowing terms how his idea is superior to the other.

Another favorite spot of The Bragger is the teachers' room. He'll sidle up to where a discussion is going on among a few other teachers, and it isn't long before he has broken into the conversation and is pouring forth his own great ideas which, according to him, the others really ought to try if they want something that really works.

The Agitator. Somewhat akin to the bragger is the agitator. He's the type of guy who is constantly running for president of the local teachers' union but never being elected because the majority of his peers fear what he might do if he were in control.

The board of education, in his eyes, is often the culprit for everything that is wrong with the school. Or the superintendent. Or the principal. Nothing is ever done right, and he's the man who is going to do something about it.

He's usually more steam than fire. He'll spout off at board of education meetings, or go storming into the principal's office to get everything off his chest. But once he does, he's usually placated until the next episode.

Strangely enough, he was a quiet, subdued, happy teacher the first three years he taught in the school system—until he acquired tenure!

The I'll-Have-It-For-You-Tomorrow Teacher. He's the fellow who never turns his reports in on time. Students have to wait for their grades. He's always late to teachers' meetings. He's never in the classroom when the class is scheduled to start. He generally arrives at school just as, or just after, the student late bell rings.

He's been docked several times for tardiness to school, but it doesn't seem to remedy his problem. Somewhere in his childhood he apparently became a "I'll have it for you tomorrow" sort of person and nothing is going to change him.

The Look-the-Other-Way Teacher. He's the teacher who takes a different route when he sees two students fighting in the hallway. Or he walks right past them and pretends not to notice. He doesn't want to "get involved." Besides, it's not *his* job to stop the fight. It's the hall monitor's or the principal's.

Even in his own classroom he'll avoid at all costs noticing any infraction of rules, because if he sees it, he'll have to take some action, and that's just too much trouble.

The Goof-Offs. The army has them. Most businesses have them. Certainly all secondary schools have them. It, like the agitator, is a disease that manifests itself strangely enough just after the teacher receives tenure.

For some reason physical education teachers seem to be afflicted with it more often than other teachers. They're down in the boiler room talking with a janitor while their classes are in the locker room getting dressed. Or they're out in the hall conversing with another teacher while their classes are inside playing volley ball.

Subject teachers aren't immune to it. You can see them if you look through the window in the door. He's at his desk reading the paper while the kids are doing written work. A couple of students raise their hands for help, but they soon give up because he can't see through the newspaper.

The Loner. He's easy to pick out from the rest of the faculty members. He sits off by himself during teachers' meeting and seldom if ever has anything to say. He never stops to talk to anyone as he's walking down the hall. He eats by himself in the teachers' lunchroom. And in the teachers' rooms he's too busy correcting papers or writing lesson plans to have time to have a chat with any of the other teachers. He's not a part of the team.

The Sloppy Dresser. It's true, of course, that teachers now are permitted to dress more informally than they could forty or fifty years ago. But in every faculty there's one that stands out. He wears dirty blue jeans, a faded dirty shirt with a frayed collar. His toes may be protruding from the tips of his shoes, and he never wears socks. He hasn't shaved in several days. He sets a poor example for his students.

Usually his classroom is as disorderly as his clothes. By the end of the day one can wade through the papers that litter the floor. Supplementary texts are strewn about the tables and bookshelves where they were stored; some have fallen on the floor. There are paper airplanes on top of the fluorescent light fixtures. At best there may be a few square inches of his desk which are not covered with file folders, students' work, and other unidentifiable papers, some torn, some crumpled, some yellow with age.

If the principal were to try to decipher this teacher's marking book, as sometimes happens during the summer recess when a student's mark is in doubt, he would need a magnifying glass and hours of patience to read through the scribbles, the cross outs, the erasure that never quite made it, and the pencil smudges that obliterate parts of pages.

The Quiet "Nipper." He hides the bottle in his desk drawer and keeps the drawer locked when he's not in the room. Every half hour or so he slyly pours himself a jiggerful and, when he thinks no one in the class is looking, gulps it down. Of course, every student in the room is secretly watching, and everyone in the school knows about it, including the principal. But he's powerless to do much about it because he can't get the proof he needs in order to bring charges against the teacher. There even may be a teacher or two who are taking drugs.

The "I–Don't-Know-What-Could-Have-Happened-to-Them Teacher. He's the teacher, comes the end of the school year, who can't account for half his textbooks, doesn't know where his movie projector went, is missing two student desks, and overused his paper supply by twice what he had been allotted.

The students complain to him because he hasn't returned homework or classroom work that they turned in weeks before. Sometimes these papers turn up weeks or months later, underneath one of the drawers in the teacher's desk or behind a set of texts in the bookshelf, or even at home some place.

Common Complaints Parents Make About Teachers

One of the jobs of a high school principal is to field complaints about teachers brought to him by parents. Such complaints require very sensitive handling. On the one hand, he owes his teachers a certain amount of "protection" from the "outside world" so they can teach in an atmosphere which shields them from unfounded criticism. On the other hand, if a parent has a legitimate complaint it must be thoroughly investigated, and if true, the teacher must be reprimanded; if serious enough, dismissal proceedings must be initiated.

Many parents believe that it's useless to make a complaint, because no matter how much evidence is presented the principal will "protect his own." This may be true in some schools, but the vast majority of principals I know are fair-minded and will not shield a teacher if he is in the wrong. The belief has come about, I believe, because many parents think that rumor and innuendos and tales brought home by their son or daughter are proof of a teacher's wrongdoing.

Listed below are eight complaints of a minor nature which are commonly brought to a principal's attention:

1. *"My son's teacher never assigns any homework. Tommy comes home night after night and when I ask him why he isn't doing his homework, he tells me he doesn't have any."*

Sometimes this is a legitimate complaint; most of the time Tommy either doesn't plan to do the homework or he expects to do it the next day in one of his other classes which meets before the assignment is due.

If it's a legitimate complaint or not, the principal must follow through and report back to the parent. He will schedule a meeting with Tommy's teacher and ask the teacher to bring along samples of homework assignments which the teacher has collected during the past few weeks.

The principal will ask the teacher how promptly Tommy hands in his assignments. Often he'll discover that Tommy rarely hands in any work, and the teacher will show the principal his grade book to verify this. The principal will probably ask the teacher to leave the grade book with him until after his meeting with Tommy's parents.

On the other hand, there could be incidents when the teacher has been remiss in assigning any homework. Sometimes, there is an acceptable reason: the type of work being done in class does not lend itself to a homework assignment, or the homework is a long-term project, due in several weeks or perhaps even a month.

And there are times when the teacher has either been negligent or lazy and has not made assignments. In such cases the principal will advise the teacher that homework assignments are required as part of school policy and that henceforth at least two or three will be made each week.

The principal will then report back to the parent and admit that, indeed, no homework had been assigned by the teacher, but that starting immediately the situation would be remedied and that the parent should notify the school if such a change does not take place.

2. *"My daughter says she hands in her work on time, but when it's returned to her it hasn't been corrected and she hasn't been given a grade."*

This is one of the most difficult complaints to resolve. It's very difficult to explain to a parent that a teacher cannot possibly go over in detail every paper that is turned in. Some teachers average several hundred pages of handwritten work each day and they are assigned one preparation period, in which they must prepare for the next day's lessons, correct tests, prepare reports and average grades.

Most teachers select one or two of the most important papers each week and spend time reading and marking them. The rest of the papers receive a check mark, indicating that they have been turned in and recorded in the marking book. If a paper has not been turned in, it is graded as a zero.

There are teachers who seldom if ever grade students' papers with anything more than a casual glance or two. There's the often quoted explanation of this type of teacher: "He throws the papers up the stairs. The heaviest ones go the farthest and they get an 'A'. The bottom ones get an 'F'."

3. *"The teacher is constantly picking on my child. Others in the class do the same thing and they don't get punished."*

This is usually the story the son or daughter brings home to his parents when he's been kept after school or suspended. And too many parents are inclined to accept their child's word and go fuming to the principal claiming an injustice has been done. Most of the time the parent finally sees the light and accepts the teacher's explanation.

This is not to say that some teachers don't have pets. It is human nature to have likes and dislikes, and some teenagers just stand out above the rest in intelligence and personality. But the smart teacher is careful to hide any preferences he may have for a particular student, because nothing can cause more resentment from the rest of the class—against the teacher *and* against the favored student. Such resentment gradually will cause a deterioration of the class morale and discipline.

4. *"My Daughter hasn't been assigned a textbook in her social studies class. How can she learn anything if she doesn't use a textbook?"*

This parent may not realize it, but that social studies teacher is doing his daughter a service by not assigning a single text. Undoubtedly he is making use of a number of supplementary texts and is probably assigning research work as well. In social studies, science, and literature, confining a class to a single text limits the field of study and prevents the students from getting the viewpoint of a number of different writers.

5. *"Last year my son got all A's in science. This year he's only receiving C's. Why is Mr. Simmons such a hard marker? He discourages kids from trying."*

Perhaps last year's science teacher was too *easy* a marker! Or perhaps this year his son is not putting forth the same effort as he did a year ago. Or maybe this year's science course is more difficult. Just because the boy isn't receiving as high a grade as he did the year before doesn't imply that this year's teacher is a hard marker.

Different teachers have different standards, there's no denying that. Not all judges mete out the same punishment for the same crime. Different states have different penalties for the same offense. And in our schools it's not possible to expect each teacher to mark with the same standards.

6. *"My daughter is very bright. She just isn't being challenged in Mrs. Clemson's class and she's bored."*

This is a complaint that often results when classes have been heterogeneously grouped, a condition which is most likely to occur in high schools of limited enrollment. When a teacher is confronted with a group of children whose I.Q.'s range from about 85 to 130 or higher, he is faced with the problem of gearing his lessons so that the low I.Q. students are not left behind and the higher I.Q. students are not bored by the repetition.

There is no easy solution except to regroup the students homogeneously or, better yet, to place the brighter students on individualized instruction while the teacher works with the slower students, and to use some of the top students as tutors for the poorer ones. But it takes a creative, dedicated teacher to put such a plan into action, and most teachers are inclined to take the easy route and hope that the brighter students will bear with him.

7. *"The teacher never lets my son go to the boys' room or get a drink of water."*

Every day a typical high school teacher teaches approximately one hundred and fifty students. If each of the students requested permission to go to the boys' or girls' room, bedlam would exist. But if one student is given permission, then in all fairness the other one hundred and forty-nine should also receive the same privilege. As a result, most teachers refuse permission to all students except in the case of an emergency.

How can the teacher be sure it's an emergency? He can't. He has to use his intuition and he has to know the reputation of the student making the request. A student who is always trying to "pull something over" on his teachers would probably be refused permission to go. On the other hand, a reliable student who seldom makes any requests to leave the room and who tells the teacher she is "in that time of the month" would receive prompt permission.

If a student persists in his request and makes dire predictions of what might happen if he isn't allowed to go, the teacher has the option of turning the decision over to the principal or the school nurse.

The complaints discussed above are, for the most part, superficial and easily solved. There are, however, several serious complaints that occur from time to time that must be treated with the utmost urgency:

(1) **The Use of Corporal Punishment by the Teacher.** There are a number of teachers in the work force of our nation's schools who, either out of frustration or anger, resort to some form of corporal punishment to solve their discipline problems.

The use of corporal punishment varies from state to state. Many states prohibit any form. Others permit spankings by the principal. Still others require that a parent be present when the punishment is administered by the principal. I know of no states which permit a teacher to use corporal punishment in the classroom in front of the rest of the class.

When a teacher strikes out in anger, it is usually because the discipline in the room has deteriorated to the point where the class is out of control. He had tried every other conceivable means to restore order, and those failing, he had in a moment of anger and frustration, lashed out with his hands or fists.

There is, of course, no excuse for this to happen. In part, the responsibility lies with the administration who should have been aware of what was happening. Classroom discipline does not deteriorate overnight, and if the principal had been circulating through his school, which is a part of his job, he would have become aware of what was going on in that classroom.

The teacher who is guilty of using corporal punishment must, of course, be brought up on charges and he must be relieved of his teaching duties, with pay, until a determination is made. In most states, the board of education is the first body to hear the case. From here it may go to the state department of education or to the courts, depending upon the state where it occurs.

If found guilty, dismissal is the usual punishment, with a revocation of the teacher's license.

(2) **Teachers Accused of Sex Offenses.** During the past twenty years there has been a marked increase in the number of cases involving teachers who have made sexual advances upon their students. Perhaps the increase is due because students are more inclined to voice a complaint than they were several decades ago. Or the increase could be a result of the sexual freedom which has become a part of our society today.

Whatever the reason, when a teacher is accused of performing a sexual act upon a student, the teacher must be removed from the classroom immediately and remain apart from all students until he is either cleared of the charges or found guilty, in which case the board of education will have no problem terminating his contract.

Case Studies of Teachers I Have Known. (Only the names have been changed.)

Case Study Number One: Malcolm Dudley, male, 43 years old, Caucasian, married, five children, tenured, twelve years in the school system, science major. For the past five years he has been assigned classes in biology.

It's fifth period. The late bell has just rung. Mr. Dudley is seated at his desk surrounded by four girls who are telling him about the dance they attended the night before. The rest of the class is scattered about the room in small groups, talking. Three boys and a girl have taken their seats. The girl is working on an assignment for another class. The three boys have drawn their desks together and are looking at a girlie magazine.

Mr. Dudley and the four girls continue their chat. Finally, about seven or eight minutes after the late bell rang, the girls leave the front of the room and join up with one of the groups of students near the rear bulletin board.

Mr. Dudley continues at his seat for a few more minutes and then leisurely gets to his feet, turns about, picks up a piece of chalk and writes on the board: "Assignment for today. Read Chapter Eleven and answer questions 1, 3, 5, 6, 7 and 10 at the end of the chapter."

The students continue their small-group discussions. Finally Mr. Dudley picks up a pen and begins to tap methodically on his desk. A few of the students look his way and he points toward their desk, indicating that he wants them to be seated.

Gradually, after several more taps on the desk and several vocal appeals, the entire class is seated. Mr. Dudley then calls their attention to the class assignment he has placed on the blackboard.

Three boys and two girls open their texts and begin to read the assignment. Three other girls open their books, but instead of reading, begin to converse across the aisle. The boys who had been watching the girlie magazine, size up their chances of continuing, and finally decide that the coast is clear, so they pull their desks together at the rear of the room and place the magazine on one of the boy's laps where Mr. Dudley can't see it.

But Mr. Dudley isn't concerned about the boys and their magazine. He has moved to the side aisle where three girls are looking at photos taken over the past weekend when one of the girls went on a canoe trip. Mr. Dudley asks to look at the pictures, and the girls oblige. He makes a comment about one of the pictures and the girls break out laughing. The rest of the class stops what they are doing momentarily to look over at the girls and Mr. Dudley, wondering what had happened that was so funny.

Mr. Dudley walks away from the girls and goes to the front of the room where he tells the class to stop what they're doing and get busy on the assignment.

A few comply. The rest continue what they are doing.

At the end of the period Mr. Dudley tells the class to put their papers in the wire basket on his desk on their way out. Six students turn in papers. One boy says to Mr. Dudley, "I'll turn it in tomorrow, O.K.?" and Mr. Dudley tells the boy, sure, any time will be all right.

The next day the same class has Mr. Dudley for a biology laboratory. After five or six minutes most of the class is seated at their lab tables. Mr. Dudley goes into the supply room next to the lab and brings out several trays of frog specimens. He places them on his desk.

"Do the experiment on page 28 in your lab manuals," he tells the class, "and when you're finished with the experiment, fill in all the blanks in the manual. Everything you need is right here on my desk. I'll be back in a few minutes."

He leaves the room and makes his way down to the teachers' lounge where he lights up a cigarette and gets a cold drink from the vending machine.

Ten minutes before the end of the period he returns to the lab. He's greeted, upon entering, with a chorus of complaints from the class. They couldn't understand the directions in the lab manual. There weren't enough frog specimens to go around. Jim Mason was going around bothering everyone who was trying to work.

Mr. Dudley gives them a casual shrug of his shoulders and tells them not to worry. He'll assume everyone in the room performed the experiment satisfactorily.

At the end of the marking period, three-quarters of the class received A's and the rest B's. Not one student complained.

Not until they got to college and had to repeat the course.

Case Study Number Two: Mary Louise Green, female, 51 years old, black, widowed, no children, tenured, twenty-eight years in the school system, social studies teacher.

Mrs. Green arrives at school at 7:00 A.M. every morning, which gives her an hour before her first class to lay out the books she plans to use during the day, have students' papers ready to return, and place on the blackboard material she wants her classes to copy in their notebooks.

The first bus load of students arrives at a quarter to eight. By this time Mrs. White has finished her preparations and she stands outside her classroom and greets students as they go by on their way to their lockers. Many of them stop for a few minutes to chat with her. She asks Lisa how her mother is getting along in the hospital.

Then she stops Benny to make sure he's done his homework for Mr. Smythington. She's all smiles when he tells her that he has. Yesterday Gus Smythington had told her that Benny would fail for the year if he didn't get his work done on time. Mrs. Green is very interested in Benny's future because she taught Benny's mother twenty-five years ago.

She calls Anthony over, places a motherly arm about his shoulder, and tells him that kissing one's sweetheart is something one does in private, not in the hallway, because kissing someone whom one loves is a very special thing and it isn't done where everyone can watch. Anthony grins sheepishly, thanks Mrs. Green and tells her that she's right and he won't do it again.

At eight o'clock Mrs. White takes attendance in her home room, compliments Julia on how nice she looks, passes out some chocolate chip cookies she made the evening before and makes the class promise they won't eat them before lunch time.

Homeroom ends at 8:07, and four minutes later the twenty-nine students of her first period class have filed into the room and have taken their seats. Mrs. Green stands by the door as they enter and has a few words to say to most of them as they pass by. John Raccini sneaks up to her desk when she isn't looking and places an apple on it.

Mrs. Green doesn't have to ask her class to be quiet or to settle down. As soon as she moves from the door, everyone stops talking and turns his attention to what she is about to say. They know that today, like every day since school opened, her class will be interesting and challenging.

During the next few minutes Mrs. Green explains the four topics she had previously placed on the blackboard: "The Great Depression," "The Roosevelt Era," "Hitler's Rise to Power and His Threat to the World," and "World War II." She explains that she would like to divide the class into four groups, each group to take one of the topics, research it as a group, and present their findings to the class in an interesting and novel way.

She has written the name of each student on a slip of paper and has placed the slips in a bowl. Now she tells the class that the first seven names that are drawn will form the first committee, the second seven another committee, and so forth until all four committees have been chosen.

Simon raises his hand and Mrs. Green tells him to go ahead, tell her what's on his mind. "You've been teaching us about democracy, Mrs. Green," he says. "Wouldn't it be better if *we* selected the committees?"

She smiles. "I was afraid for a time no one would challenge me," she says. "Yes, Simon, you are right. I purposely used this method of selecting the committees to see if you, the class, have learned anything at all this year about how nations, groups—and individuals—have their democratic rights taken away from them. I would have been very disappointed if no one had challenged me."

Mrs. Green is most often the last teacher to leave the building at the close of school. After seventh period, students who don't have to catch a bus just naturally congregate in her room. Some play chess in the back of the room; others stand around Mrs. Green's desk and talk with her.

Sometimes a student will wait patiently until all the others have left so he can speak to her alone. About a personal problem, most often. She's always ready to listen and to help out, if that's what's expected of her.

Some Saturdays she comes to school and does volunteer work helping youngsters who are deficient in reading and mathematics.

Evaluation

Rate each of the following statements by placing an x beneath the appropriate number. Then connect the x's with a continuous line to form a graph.

1   2   3   4   5

- The high school teachers in my community's school are proficient in their knowledge of subject matter.
- Teachers are given adequate time to prepare their lessons and correct papers.
- Teachers perform a minimum of duties outside the classroom.
- The high school in my community sponsors a variety of clubs and extracurricular activities and allots time during the school day for them to meet.
- Supervision is provided during lunch time and in the hallways.
- The high school schedules at least one fire drill each month.
- Teachers are given released time to attend meetings and to work on curricula.
- The administration works with teachers to correct irksome personality problems.
- The administration listens to and acts upon all complaints made by parents.
- The administration and the board of education take all measures allowable under the laws of the state and nation to rid itself of undesirable, unproductive teachers.

Chapter Eight

SUPPLIES AND TEXTS

TEXTS

There is a growing tendency in both the elementary and secondary schools to do away with the single text in favor of a variety of single copies of supplementary books. Educators cite a number of advantages:

1. A single text issued to all students in a class restricts the scope of information available to the class to one author's extent of knowledge and point of view.

The availability of many books in each classroom provides young readers with many points of view and can give greater in-depth discussion.

2. One text may be deficient in certain areas. Example: In studying the Indians of North America, the author may give a great deal of weight and space to a discussion of the Indians of the eastern part of the country, but very little discussion of the Indians of the West or the Eskimos of the North.

In place of the single text, four or five titles of perhaps five or ten copies each can be bought which, together, give a far wider view of Indian life.

3. Because many texts become out-of-date within four or five years, purchasing a single text becomes an expensive venture when a hundred or more copies (thirty to a classroom) must be discarded before they have been worn out.

While it's true that single-copy texts become outdated equally as fast, the number of copies is significantly fewer.

4. The use of a single text places the teacher in a position where she is "tied down" to that text; creativity in teaching methods is often curtailed as a result.

5. A classroom supplied with thirty, forty, or fifty individual titles all selected to provide reference material for the subject content of the course of study, provide the students with far greater in-depth material than would be available to them from a single text.

131

6. The multitext approach to teaching mandates that students learn the techniques of research, note-taking, compiling information, and rewriting in their own words the information they have assimilated.

Even in the primary grades teachers are relying more and more on a number of reading books rather than one "primer," and have found that, as a result, children are acquiring a greater range of vocabulary than when they were restricted to a single text.

This is a distinct break from the policies in effect during the fifties, sixties, and even into the seventies when a single text was a "must" in the elementary school reading program. Not only was a single text required at each grade level, but a child was required to move through an integrated series year after year.

Many adults who were children during these decades will recall with little enthusiasm their introduction to reading. The Scott Foresman series of elementary school texts remained first in sales among all the publishers of "primers" in the schools of this country following World War II. As a child moved through the primary grades, he read about Dick and Jane and Spot again and again in one dull episode after another.

Experimentation has proved that most children can profit from a wide selection of readers of varying difficulty. A child knows almost immediately upon picking up a book if the vocabulary is too difficult and he will put it down and select an easier one, or will seek help to sound out the words with which he is not familiar.

A scientifically structured series of texts, in which each subsequent book adds a measured number of new words to the child's vocabulary, has not been proven to be either necessary nor beneficial.

In mathematics, too, in the primary grades, several texts and several workbooks, have proven advantageous, particularly when each of the texts is written for a different level of difficulty. The teacher can then move a fast learner along at a quicker pace, or have available workbooks with repetitive exercises for the slower learner who needs additional practice.

In schools where the single-text concept is still being practiced, I have seen storerooms where the shelves are lined with hundreds of copies of a text, most of the books hardly worn, purchased by an administrator because of a fast-talking salesman who took the administrator out to dinner and convinced him that the text was just what his third-, or fourth-, or fifth-grade teacher wanted. But the third-, fourth-, or fifth-grade teacher had other ideas. It wasn't at all the text she wanted for her classes. In fact, she had made a budget request at the end of the previous year for an entirely different book.

All texts, workbooks and supplemental texts must be selected by the teachers who will be using them. This is a cardinal rule by which all administrators must live. If a principal, coordinator of elementary instruction, or secondary school department head have reason to distrust the judgment of a teacher in her selection of a text, series of reference books, or workbooks, a conference with that teacher will usually straighten out the problem.

The cost of textbooks, workbooks, and supplemental texts is a large item in the budget of all boards of education, and many boards are concerned whether the money is being spent to the best advantage. Often it is felt that texts are not used to their full life, that after a few years these books are gathering dust in the book room.

This is, unfortunately, often the case. Perhaps a new teacher has been hired who feels the text is inadequate. Or it may be that the course of study has been rewritten and this text no longer qualifies. But more often than not, the text has been abandoned because newer, more up-to-date, and better written texts have come along.

Science and social studies texts become outdated the fastest; mathematics and English literature books have a long life and generally are discarded only because they have become too worn to be used for another term.

The extensive use of color plates during the past twenty years has greatly increased the cost of many textbooks. Many educators believe that publishers have gone overboard; many of the illustrations are frivolous and add little to the understanding of the text. Some books contain more illustrations than printed matter.

There is a growing tendency among some boards of education to purchase paperbacks instead of hard cover texts and supplemental texts in the belief that money is saved by doing so. This may be true in cases where the books are to be used for a single term and then discarded—a situation which rarely if ever happens. But for texts that will be in use for a longer period of time, hard cover books are the best selection.

Students, particularly those in the middle and secondary schools, have a habit of curling paperback books until they are no longer serviceable, and they are able to accomplish this task in the matter of a few minutes. If you ask them why they did it, they will usually tell you they were unaware of what they were doing!

A word should be said about teacher-control of the books assigned to him at the beginning of the year. An efficient school keeps an inventory of every book purchased. The most common system for keeping track of a book is to assign it a number which is written inside the cover, usually as part of a rubber stamp imprint which also provides space for the student to write his name, date, and condition of the book at the time he received it.

The teacher then records the number of the book in her grading book and at the end of the year checks this number against the book which the student turns in. If the student attempts to turn in a book that was not assigned to him, credit is given to the student to whom the book was originally lent.

This system is applicable only to schools which use the single-text system. For schools that have moved to the multitext system, keeping track of the flow of books is far more complicated.

Under the multitext system a book is borrowed by a student for an undeterminable number of days or weeks—until he has finished the assignment for which he has borrowed it. In many cases, particularly during his high school years, he may find a need for several books or as many as a half dozen at one time. Some of the books he borrows may come from the supplementary texts in his classroom, and others from the school's media center.

To keep these books separated and to make sure they are returned requires a well-organized and well-defined system. All classroom teachers should agree on a uniform method to make it easier for students to follow.

There are a number of systems that have proven effective. The one most widely in use resembles the method used by most public libraries: a cardboard pocket pasted inside the rear cover of each book contains a card with the name of the book and lines for the student to write his name. The card is turned over to the teacher who holds it until the book is returned. Some teachers assign the job of collecting these cards to a reliable student in each class.

This system is practically foolproof *if* the supplementary texts are placed in a locked closet and opened only when a student wishes to make a selection. If books are not locked up, students will borrow them with the intention of using them a few minutes and then replacing them. But the bell rings or someone distracts their attention and the books leave the room unwittingly and are never returned.

Another way a teacher may lose many of her supplementary texts results when they are distributed at the beginning of a period for work in class and not thoroughly checked out at the close of the period to make sure that all copies have been returned. Although it will require additional work, it is a good practice to record the number of the book against each student's name even when the books are to be used for a single period. There can be no argument then as to which student withheld a book.

The modern elementary school and the high school have come to depend heavily on the workbook as a source of educationally sound material for use in the teaching of language arts, social studies, science and mathematics classes. These workbooks have been developed by authorities in the field, usually by teachers who have had years of experience in the field and have developed these teaching aids through actual classroom trial and error. Workbooks save a teacher hours of preparation time, and usually result in a superior teaching device.

However, some boards of education are reluctant to spend the money required to supply each student with a copy in each of his major subjects. A study I made a few years back indicated that the workbooks actually cost no more than the cost of paper, ditto masters, and the teacher's time in preparing teacher-made work sheets.

Many schools have a policy that a workbook must be reused a second time, thereby requiring the initial user to copy the material plus his answer. Again, the cost of the paper needed for the student to do the assignment probably costs the board as much, if not more, than the paper on which the workbook has been printed. The only redeeming feature of requiring a student to rewrite the material is that the student receives reinforcement in his writing skills.

SUPPLIES

Any educational materials which are expended during the course of a school year are considered supplies, funds for which are generally contained in a separate budget item. In a large school district the amount can be extensive, and it is here that many boards try to cut expenses, claiming that teachers are wasteful and extravagant.

These charges are partly true. Perhaps it's a sign of our times to use more of everything than is required to do the job. Back in our forefather's day, schools saved every scrap of paper not written on; students were required to use the back of every sheet of paper. Bits of colored construction paper were carefully retrieved after the class had finished a project and put away for the next time.

Today I have seen high school students pick up five or six pieces of white ink paper, write a sentence or two, crumple up the piece of paper and go on to the next piece, sometimes using as many as a half dozen sheets before completing the composition.

Teachers are often culprits, too. A recent bulletin board display used about thirty sheets of red construction paper as a background for the lettering and posters thumbtacked over them. When the display was finally dismantled, the construction paper, without a single blemish, was tossed into the basket with the rest of the material.

Ream after ream of mimeograph paper and ditto paper are wasted every day in the typical high school. Teachers tend to run off far more copies than are required. Janitors at the end of the day incinerate hundreds of unused copies of tests and worksheets.

The extent and variety of materials required by teachers grows with each passing year. School supply catalogs have expanded as teacher demands increased. Items which teachers and their classes formerly would construct for themselves are now purchased ready-made.

Here is a typical requisition from a third-grade teacher for a two-month's supply of classroom materials:

5 quarts poster paint, green
5 quarts poster paint, orange
5 quarts of poster paint, yellow
3 quarts of poster paint, black
3 quarts of poster paint, white
5 quarts of poster paint, blue
Poster paper, 100 sheets per package, 10 × 15, 15 white, 15 green,
    15 blue, 10 black, 15 yellow, 12 orange, 5 flesh, 5 lavender
5 gross student pencils #2
2 boxes chalk
20 reams white lined composition paper
20 reams yellow lined composition paper
15 reams unlined arithmetic paper
30 boxes of crayons, 15 colors to the box
30 boxes of colored pencils, 12 colors to the box
20 pairs of scissors
5 rolls of Kraft paper, 30″ wide
20 rulers
10 boxes of thumb tacks

8 boxes of paper clips
Stickers, 30 each of Thanksgiving, Christmas, Valentine's Day, Fourth
  of July, Animals, Birds, Fish, and Pets
10 quarts of paste
1 gross of file folders, legal size
30 wood blocks for carving
30 Xacto carving kits
2 reams of graph paper
10 Magic Marker sets, 5 colors
5 cellophane tape w/dispenser

The principal, upon receiving this request, called the teacher to his office to ask her the following questions: Why did she need 20 scissors — she received 30 pair with her last requisition? Her reply: the children lose them. How? I don't know. I guess they get tossed into the waste basket.

How could she possibly use twenty reams of white lined paper, plus twenty reams of yellow lined, *and* another fifteen reams of arithmetic paper? Did she realize that twenty reams equaled ten thousand sheets of paper — over three hundred sheets for *each* child in *two months?*

Yes, she realized that was a lot of paper, but that's how much she had ordered the previous requisition and the children had used it all up somehow. And she had given a couple of reams to Mrs. Eggart who had run out.

And what on earth did she do with all that poster paint?

She planned on having the kiddies make a giant mural and she figured that's how much paint they would need to cover it.

The principal gave up and ordered all the material. If he had refused to order any part of her order he might have jeopardized her ability to effectively teach her class. How could he know for sure whether her request was realistic or not unless he spent the next two months in her room making careful note as to how each piece of paper was used and where the scissors disappeared to?

To avoid such extravagance, many school districts require that each teacher turn in a form every few months on which is indicated where and how the bulk of the supplies was expended.

But the supplies required to keep a modern high school going for a year far exceeds anything the elementary school requires, both in number and cost. Besides the ordinary paper and pencil supplies, here are a few examples of the more important items listed by department:

For the science department: Dozens of different chemicals, live and preserved biological specimens, test tube and beaker replacements.

For the home economics department: needles, threads, patterns, food supplies, various dress materials.

For the industrial arts department: wood and metal paints, sandpaper, lumber, replacement blades, metals, photographic chemicals and films, offset inks, offset paper, offset plates, auto paints, drafting supplies.

For the art department: paints, drawing paper, brushes, molding clay, drawing pencils, silk screen materials, raffia, plaster of paris, caning, fixatives, charcoal pencils.

In any school system the task of preparing bids for supplies is a demanding job. If the desired article is not carefully and fully described, suppliers, to keep their bids competitively low, will offer an inferior product and under the laws of most states, the board of education would be required to accept it.

In a typical order for ten typewriters, electric, IBM Selectric or Equal, the use of the words *or equal* can result in a board of education having to accept an inferior product or having to go to court to prove that the typewriters the lowest bidder is proposing to deliver, do not measure up to the named product.

Providing school supplies to the thousands of school districts across the country is big business, and every year "fly-by-night" companies enter the market, underprice the established companies, and then deliver shoddy merchandise just before the opening of school. At that late date, most boards of education would hesitate to refuse delivery. And some of these fly-by-nighters probably would go bankrupt prior to the opening of school and the school would receive no delivery at all.

Evaluation

Rate each of the following statements by placing an x beneath the appropriate number. Then connect all the x's with a continuous line to form a graph.

1   2   3   4   5

- The schools in your community do not rely entirely on a single text.
- An adequate supply of supplementary texts is provided for each classroom.
- Research techniques are begun in the early grades and carried through into high school.

- In the primary grades no single "primer" or series of readers is used.
- All texts, workbooks, and supplemental texts are selected by the teachers who will use them.
- All teachers have put into practice a foolproof method of checking out supplemental texts.
- All supplemental texts are under lock and key except while being used.
- Workbooks are widely used in all grades.
- Adequate supplies are furnished to all teachers.
- A system to prevent waste of supplies is operating in all schools.
- Bidding for supplies is carried out in an efficient, businesslike manner.

Chapter Nine

ELEMENTARY AND SECONDARY
ATHLETIC PROGRAMS

The Question Still Hasn't Been Answered—Are America's Public Schools too Athletically-Oriented?

A board of education recently appropriated $235,000.00 to install lights for the high school football field so night games could be played in addition to the Saturday afternoon games. At the same meeting the board voted down a motion to provide computers for the elementary school mathematics program. Their reason: the children would receive computer instruction when they reached the high school.

Another board of education allocated $122,000 from the capital outlay account to tear up the cinder running track and install astroturf because one of the board members had heard from his son that the school's star miler had refused to run track any longer because he considered the cinder track inferior.

These may or may not be isolated cases, but they are representative of the way many boards of education think. It must be remembered that boards of education in most states are made up of lay people, many of them men who have a passion for athletics and a very poor understanding of the academic workings of a school. It is natural that their enthusiasm would be vented in the direction that they understand the best.

There are many in this country, including lay people and educators as well, who believe that in certain ways the athletic program in some schools has become the tail that wags the dog. The particular sport which receives the lion's share of the criticism varies according to the section of the country. Football, by far, is the biggest villain of these critics, with basketball in close second. It isn't the sport itself that is receiving the criticism; in most instances it's the manner in which this sport overshadows the academic programs of the school. Examples cited by these critics:

Team players are excused from the last three periods of the day whenever they must travel to another school for a game. Teachers are required to write up a brief summary of what transpired in class and the homework assignment, and these summaries are duplicated and given to the team players at the close of the game.

All boys and girls who are a member of the first squad of any sport are excused from taking physical education while their sport is in season. During this excused period they are assigned to a study hall, or in some schools, they are permitted to leave school grounds if they have parental permission.

A football player who is failing one or more subjects is permitted to play ball if the team is short a player for his position.

Proportionately, more money is spent on athletics than on the academic subjects. This proportion is figured by comparing the time a student is in his academic classes to the time he spends in practice and in the actual games, and the number of students benefiting from the sports programs compared to the number in the regular academic program.

It should be emphasized that critics who have attacked the American elementary and high school athletic programs are not advocating that all sports be taken out of the school program; they criticize how the program is run, what objectives it serves, and its importance in the entire educational process.

The chart below cites arguments for and against the athletic programs as they now exist:

THOSE WHO FAVOR THE ATHLETIC PROGRAM AS IT NOW IS RUN STATE:	THOSE WHO BELIEVE REFORM IS DUE, STATE:
Promotes sportsmanship; teaches boys and girls to play the game fairly and squarely and to abide by the rules of the game.	Teaches children that winning is all-important no matter how it is attained.
Encourages the "competitive" spirit which will carry over into later life and bring success in business and in their personal life.	Many children are not emotionally equipped to handle competitiveness nor to stand the pressures of maintaining a winning streak.
Builds up "teamwork" and "leadership," qualities on which America was built.	America today needs fewer leaders and more followers.
Many high school sports make a profit for the board of education	Schools aren't in the business to make money, but to educate children.
The public enjoys watching inter-scholastic sports.	Schools aren't in existence to entertain the public.

Parents want their children to be athletic and to participate in team sports.	Parents are really only interested in seeing their child's team win.
Many sports are carried over into adulthood and provide both relaxation and a healthful activity	Yes, sports such as golf, tennis, and handball are the kind of athletics we are in favor of.
Athletics build strong, healthy bodies.	Many lifelong disabilities are caused by football, soccer, and basketball injuries.
Athletic activities build school spirit.	Not *school* spirit but *athletic spirit,* a kind of pseudo school spirit.
	Too many schools place more emphasis on their athletic program than on their educational program.
	Sports programs — school, Little League, Pop Warner, Etc. — take too much of the child's time away from normal childhood activities.

It is not the intention to decide here which "camp" is correct. Unfortunately, it finally boils down to a matter of opinion — the sports-minded American against the academic-minded. Probably the answer is somewhere in between.

Some Benefits and Pitfalls of Athletic Programs

The elementary schools have a tendency to begin several of the more strenuous sports too early. Doctors advise that children in the first three or four years of elementary school are not ready physically to engage in contact sports.

Soccer should be left for the upper elementary grades. Touch football can start around the sixth grade. Volleyball and similar games can be played by third graders. Contact football should be left for the high school years.

The tendency for elementary schools to introduce interscholastic meets should be examined further. Many educators believe that children below the seventh grade are not ready emotionally and psychologically for the intense rivalry and competitive spirit which interschool games produce in a youngster. Yet many elementary schools across the country, over the past ten or fifteen years, have engaged in an intercommunity league that encompasses as many as fifteen or twenty school districts and, in some cases, requires a team to travel as much as twenty to thirty miles to meet their opponent. Often, when asked the reason for so demanding a schedule, the answer will invariably be something to the effect that the high school needs its incoming freshmen well-trained in order to compete against other school districts.

One of the reasons often cited when asked, "What in your estimation is the single-most benefit of an athletic program?" the answer is likely to stress the fact that athletics takes the kid off the street and keeps him out of trouble. This statement is probably true if we are talking about the youngster who has never been in trouble but has the potential to get into trouble if he is not properly supervised and if he is not provided with activities that are interesting and challenging. On the other hand, if we are talking about the type of boy or girls who has already reached the stage where he has been in trouble with the law, it is highly questionable whether any athletic program—or any after school program of any type—will reach him.

Examine carefully the type of child seriously engaged in intramural sports and rarely if ever will you find one who has been in trouble with the law or who is roaming the streets without supervision. The reasons are evident: First, that type of youngster would never sign up to play on the team, because he knows ahead of time that he could not abide by the rules and regulations laid down by the coaches, rules which are necessary if the team is to become a unified, working unit. And second, should this youngster for some reason be coerced into joining up, he would soon disrupt the team's efforts to the point where the coach would find it essential to remove him from the squad.

But on the other hand, it is evident that a well-run, balanced athletic program is an essential, beneficial part of any elementary or high school program. Athletic awards and trophies remain displayed in many a home long after the recipient has left his adolescent years and has become an adult, proving the importance that person has placed on athletics.

Typical Athletic Programs for Elementary and Secondary Schools

Athletic programs in the elementary school should promote the following objectives:

1. To teach boys and girls the basics for a number of sports and to acquaint them with the rules of the game for all popular sports of the day.

The reason many children in the upper grades do not readily participate in sports can be traced to lack of training in the basic skills while they were in the lower grades. As their classmates surpassed them they tended to withdraw further and further from participation, particularly if their peers subjected them to belittlement and ridicule, as is so often the case with children of this age.

It is, therefore, extremely important that as children move through the grades they be given every opportunity to succeed in at least one sport. Coaches should make a special point of seeing that the youngster who is beginning to fall behind his peers be allowed every opportunity to build his skills and to taste success.

2. To develop muscular coordination by acquiring skills in many sports.

Some students are naturally more athletically inclined than others of their age. Some seem to "fill out" and develop their muscles more quickly. During the elementary school years, coaches should include as part of the pupils' training, exercises that help boys and girls develop their bodies.

With muscular development there is usually a corresponding improvement in skills, such as basket shooting, pitching, catching, and running. An observant coach takes note of which of his athletes need practice in these individual skills and assigns special training sessions for them.

3. To learn how to be a member of a team working toward a common objective; to sacrifice personal recognition for the good of the team.

Children of elementary age are naturally ego-centered. They have learned in the few years that they have been around that it's often "every man for himself", particularly if he comes from a family with a number of siblings. It is the task of the coaches to teach each child that besides being an individual he is at many times during his life also a part of a team, and that the objectives of the team momentarily take precedence over his own interests.

Unfortunately, many athletes never entirely learn this lesson and we see them "grandstanding" time after time whether it be during a game or, later in life, during a business convention or as a guest at a party.

4. To permit *all* children to participate with equal opportunity whether they show proficiency or not.

There are not many coaches who abide by this objective. Most become too engrossed in winning the game to pay much attention to the needs of some of their players with lesser ability.

This is unfortunate because the player who is lagging behind the others may be passing through a temporary period of readjustment. His eventual potential may exceed the boy or girl who, at the time, is the coach's "top player." Children do not grow evenly but in "fits and spurts," and may even experience times when they retrogress.

5. To instill in all children a love for sports.

This may well be the most important objective of them all. Love of sports and physical activity is a quality that will last well into adulthood and color the individual's quality of life. It will affect his mental and physical health and provide him with the wherewithal to spend many happy hours in the outdoors.

In high school the athletic program takes on a new meaning. By this time a student should have become proficient in the basics of a number of different sports and should have decided which sport he wishes to devote his time and energies to.

The high school coach's job now becomes one of developing each player into the best he is capable of becoming, and to help the player select a position within that sport in which he can become most adept.

For instance, when a student graduates from grammar school and has chosen baseball as the game he most wants to participate in, he in all likelihood is about equally good as a pitcher, a catcher, a first baseman or an outfielder. The high school coach must now study this player, and all the others that have come out for practice that first day of the season, and decide which position each should specialize in.

High school sports can be divided roughly into two categories: team sports and individual sports. Some fall in between the two categories. Track, for instance is primarily a one-man or one-woman sport, but the total effort of all the participants results in a final score as a team.

Team sports include: football, soccer, volleyball, field hockey, baseball, la crosse, and basketball.

Individual sports include: tennis, swimming, golf, table tennis, cross country, track, handball, and gymnastics.

All About Mixed-Sex Athletics

In the past twenty years, the courts have agreed that schools cannot bar girls from trying out for teams which had previously been open only to boys (or girls' teams not open to boys). The key words here are "to bar girls from trying out." The courts have held that a girl trying out for a boys' team was to be judged—and either rejected or admitted—with the same standards as a boy who was trying out for the same position on the squad. In other words, sexuality was not to be a determining factor, only competency.

As a result of these rulings, a number of cases have been heard in recent years after boards of education refused admission (most of them concerning girls wanting to join the football team). Much notoriety ensued, a few girls were admitted to teams, held their position for a while until the news media lost interest, and then resigned.

This does not mean that all sports must be of either one sex or the other. A number of sports lend themselves nicely to mixed participation: volley ball, for instance, or tennis, gymnastics, swimming, and table tennis, to name a few. Participation in these sports in high school by members of both sexes actually adds to the enjoyment of the game. Any sport that is played by adults with mixed teams of men and women certainly should be encouraged during a student's high school years as well.

The Role of the Athletic Director

In large school districts the athletic director is nearly always a full-time position. In smaller districts he may serve as athletic director for three or four periods a day and as a physical education teacher the remainder of the time. He may also serve as head of the physical education department.

The athletic director's office is usually situated near the gymnasium and close to the exits to the athletic fields. It may contain a window opening into the boys' locker area.

Before a board of education hires its first athletic director, the administration prepares a job description of the office, and the board approves it or makes amendments to it. This job description serves as a guideline for the administration while interview applicants to fill the position.

Following is a typical job description for a large high school:

JOB DESCRIPTION

Office of the Athletic Director

The person who fills the position of Office of Athletic Director will have the following qualifications:

1. He shall hold a master's degree in physical education or a related field.

2. He shall have served as a physical education teacher or in a closely related field for at least five years.

3. He shall be fully certified to serve as an athletic director in this state.

4. He shall have served as an assistant athletic director or as the head of a physical education department for at least two years, or shall have equivalent managerial experience in public or private education.

The duties of the athletic director are as follows:

1. He shall contact the other schools in the league and arrange for varsity and junior varsity games, set the time and place of the games for all sports in each of the three seasons, and he shall keep an accurate chart showing these matches which shall be available for review by all coaches and assistant coaches.

2. He shall arrange with the director of transportation for buses to transport the teams to all games.

3. He shall arrange for all referees and umpires for all home games.

4. He shall work with the director of buildings and grounds to keep all athletic fields in condition.

5. He shall interview and recommend to the administration and the board of education candidates for all coaching and assistant coaching positions.

6. He shall obtain from his coaches recommendations for the requisition of uniforms, supplies, and equipment for the upcoming school year and shall submit them to the administration for approval.

7. He shall keep an inventory of all uniforms, supplies, and equipment and at the end of the school year submit to the administration a list of all items which have been discarded, lost, or destroyed.

8. At the end of each sport season he shall submit to the administration an evaluation of each coach and assistant coach.

9. At the close of each school year he shall submit to the board of education, through the superintendent's office, any recommendations for changes in the athletic program for the ensuing school year.

10. He shall comply with any requests from the administration or the board of education which may be in addition to the duties listed above.

Evaluation

Rate each of the following statements by placing an x beneath the number which best describes the conditions in your community's high school. Then connect the x's with a continuous line to form a graph.

1 2 3 4 5

- The board of education balances expenditures between the academic program and the athletic program.
- Athletes receive no special privileges during the school day.
- The fundamentals of a number of sports are taught in the elementary grades.
- The elementary school has only limited interscholastic games.
- The elementary school is not a training ground to feed the high school sports program.
- The primary purposes of the athletic program in the elementary schools is to teach *all* children the basics, develop muscular coordination and to teach children to become a working member of a team.
- A number of teams in the high school are made up of both boys and girls.
- The athletic director performs his duties in accordance with the job description as given above.

Chapter Ten

EXTRACURRICULAR ACTIVITIES

The intramural athletic program covered in the last chapter is an outgrowth of the physical education curriculum; the extracurricular activities program to be discussed here is a sibling of the scholastic program.

Not much in the way of extracurricular activities occurs nor is warranted below the third or fourth grade, although many teachers include as a part of the regular school program some teaching techniques which might be considered a close relative of the extracurricular activities which later become a part of a school's program in the middle and later elementary grades.

Certain hobbies, nature projects, play acting, and some art projects which are made a part of a teacher's lesson-plans are the kind of teaching techniques which later become student interests which evolve into club membership as the child progresses through the grades.

Clubs or other extracurricular activities should be introduced gradually and on a modified scale from grades three through eight. The logical approach is to offer the activity at the time when sufficient interest is displayed by a large enough number of pupils to warrant the time and expense.

At first, the activity should meet only when there is reason to meet. If growth results then regularly scheduled meetings can be implemented.

In the upper grades of the elementary school, and in the middle school, or junior high school, club and activity sponsorship becomes a very real part of a school's educational program. This is the age when children like to "join," like to feel a part of some organization. This is the age, too, when leadership qualities are surfacing.

Many middle and elementary schools require that all students join and attend one of the clubs or organizations. Time in the school day is allocated for this purpose, usually the period just before afternoon dismissal.

There are arguments for and against compulsory club attendance.

151

Advocates state that at this age all children should acquire a hobby or interest in some subject outside the realm of the school curriculum. They believe that interests acquired at this age carry over into later life and bring many hours of happiness and satisfaction. They state further that if a child is not made aware of the many hobbies and outside interests available to him, he will never find one that he can latch on to and make a part of his life. Therefore, advocates of this philosophy generally believe that the extracurricular program should be mandatory and pupils should, during the course of a school year, be subjected to more than one activity. They believe that students should revolve through a predetermined cycle of clubs and activities. Other advocates of the compulsory attendance agree that pupils should get a sampling of a number of different activities, but they feel that the choice should be made by the pupils.

On the other hand, those educators who favor a noncompulsory extra-curricular program argue that experience has shown that when a student is forced to attend a club in which he has little or no interest, he usually becomes disruptive and, in the end, has to be removed anyway. In the meantime he has caused the teacher a great deal of anxiety and has possibly damaged the morale of the other students who have joined because they have a genuine interest in the club.

Whichever system is used, extracurricular activities are a vital and necessary part of the middle school curriculum. It would be impossible to list here all the clubs and other activities which have been sponsored by America's middle schools and in the upper grades of the elementary school, but some of the more common ones should be mentioned:

Stamp club	History club
Coin Collecting	Sewing club
Bird watching	Cooking club
Insect collecting	Manual training
Social dancing	Karate
Painting	Card games
Sculpturing	Chess
Model cars	Checkers
Model airplanes	Fishing club
Astronomy	Skating club
Soap box derby	Dance band
Debating	Marching band
Electric trains	Glee club
Baseball card collecting	Hiking and camping
Autograph collecting	Nature club

In most schools each teacher is expected to form a club at the beginning of the school year and carry it through until just before the summer vacation begins. One of the weaknesses of the extracurricular program, particularly in the middle school, comes about when there is a lack of preparation and planning for each meeting.

Middle school extracurricular activities, unlike their counterpart on the high school level, require a greater degree of teacher involvement. Children of this age are not capable of planning a meeting and carrying it out with any degree of success unless they have received considerable teacher assistance. This does not mean that the club period should be teacher dominated, but rather that the teacher should work with the student officers of the club in preparing the agendum, and be ready during the meeting to step in if the teacher feels the meeting is "falling apart," as it often will.

Unfortunately, most teachers, in my experience, are so occupied with preparing their lesson plans for the next day's classes and in correcting papers that they are apt to leave the club preparations for the last minute, or worse still, hope that the student officers have done their job. What happens? The president is sick that day, the vice-president hasn't been told what the president had planned to do, and the teacher is left with the problem, and with little if any time in which to come up with an agenda. The wise teacher has a film tucked away somewhere, or a video tape, or some form of entertainment which is related to the club's purpose which can be brought out at a moment's notice to save the day.

There is nothing that can "kill" a school club or activity faster than an ill-planned, ill-conceived, or poorly-executed meeting. Most children will forgive perhaps one meeting of this type, but if poor meetings persist, one of two things is likely to happen: the kids will not show up the next time, or if attendance is mandatory, then bedlam is likely to take place and order will be difficult to reestablish.

I've heard many a student remark, "Golly, we're on club schedule again today. Another boring hour." When remarks of this type are coming from students, it is time for the faculty to sit down and discuss the problem. Clubs and other extracurricular activities must not only be meaningful to the students who attend them, but they must be interesting and challenging, or they can actually do more harm than good. If they have become a "drag," then one of several options remains open to the faculty:

1. Reduce the frequency of the meetings to give teachers and student leaders more time to prepare for them.

2. Completely revise the types of clubs that are being offered.

3. Require that student leaders submit an outline of the agenda for the next meeting to the faculty advisor in advance of the meeting and provide the faculty advisor "free" time to meet with the student leaders.

4. Part of the problem may lie in the length of time a particular club is in existence. Some clubs are limited in the scope of their activities. Therefore, perhaps limiting each club's existence to a semester or a half semester may solve the problem.

5. Provide funds so faculty advisors may purchase or rent films, videos, or hire speakers to provide entertainment for some of the meetings.

6. Provide time and transportation for selected faculty members to visit other schools where an extracurricular activities program is carried on with success. The committee would then report back to a general teachers' meeting with its findings.

Unless an extracurricular activities program is run efficiently, and the meetings are interesting, challenging, and educational for the students who attend, the school would be better off with no program at all. The purpose of an extracurricular activities program is to channel students into worthwhile leisure time activities for adulthood, not to "turn them off" because of a mismanaged program.

High school extracurricular activities can be operated with more student control and less teacher participation than can an elementary school program. By the sophomore and junior years, students are mature enough and have had sufficient experience to take charge of their own affairs. The role of the faculty advisor now becomes one of sitting on the sidelines and being available for consultation and advice, if such is necessary.

The nature of the extracurricular activities changes somewhat, too, as will be shown in the listing that follows:

HIGH SCHOOL EXTRACURRICULAR ACTIVITIES SPONSORED BY SUBJECT DEPARTMENTS

Language Arts Department

Drama Club. Usually one of the language arts teachers has been hired because of his background and experience in coaching high school plays.

In most high schools the plays put on by the Drama Club will be the only opportunity these young people will ever have to take part in producing a play, and the only chance the people of the town have to view worthwhile dramatic and comic productions. It is my opinion that the efforts of these young actors in a good percentage of high school plays rivals the best that Broadway can produce.

All the scenery for these productions is built and painted by the students, either by a special stage production crew of the Drama club or by cooperation from the art and industrial arts department. Lighting, make-up, the changing of scenery, and sound effects are all planned and executed by the students.

For musicals the music department may supply the players or the club may have to go outside for talent. Many times a piano is all that is needed. Dance routines are usually created by the director from his observations of other renditions of the play that he has seen.

School Newspaper. Another member of the language arts department usually assumes the advisorship of the school newspaper. Today, that can be a difficult job if he has been given the responsibility to censor anything which he feels may be objectionable. On the one hand, he must be tuned to the liberal, frank thinking of modern youth. But, on the other hand, he must also consider the mores of the townspeople. More than one faculty advisor to a school newspaper has been in the middle of a city-wide controversy because he has permitted a student to print an article which is objectionable to an element of the local population.

Unfortunately, in these cases it takes only a small number of outspoken people to make life miserable for the advisor to a school newspaper. Ninety-five percent of the townspeople may feel no concern whatsoever against the article, but if the other 5 percent attend board of education meetings, come in force to the principal's office with their complaints, or make use of the town's "Letters to the Editor" section of the town paper, you can be sure that some action will be taken, and it won't be against the student who wrote the offending article.

The school newspaper is usually printed in the school's print shop on their offset machines and is either sold for a nominal price or is included in the student-government fees.

School Magazine. The publication of a school magazine is gradually disappearing from the American high school for several reasons: (1) Publishing a magazine of any consequence in size and content requires a great deal more time and energy than any faculty advisor can give — and teach five classes at the same time. (2) Experience has shown that only a very few students take the time to write material for inclusion in the publication, and usually it's the same students issue after issue. (3) A good percentage of the student body fails to read the magazine even if it is given away at no cost. Those that do read it, read only the pages devoted to humor or "personals."

Science Department

Science Fair. Science fairs have become extremely popular throughout the country and are usually supported by parents and other townspeople. Awards are made in a number of categories: biology, physics, earth science, chemistry, ecology, and astronomy to name a few. The judges are very often prominent scientists who donate their time and travel expenses because they wish to encourage young people to enter some field of science.

Astronomy Field Trips. Practically every high school sponsors an astronomy club. Part of the program of these clubs consists of nightly adventures to areas free of trees and other obstructions where students may observe the heavens through telescopes. The athletic fields make an excellent place to assemble for these excursions because they are usually devoid of trees and other obstacles.

Some schools have built observatories with orbiting telescopes, and these schools will have regularly scheduled meetings at night whenever the skies are clear.

Home Economics

Many home economics departments find that a fashion show is an ideal way to show the public the clothing that the students have made during the school year. The event is usually held in the school's auditorium and often features an accompanying food sale in the lobby during intermission and after the show.

Mathematics Department

Mathematics does not lend itself to much in the way of related extracurricular activities. I have seen a few schools where the Math Club of the high school holds a mathematics contest for pupils in the elementary grades. Prizes are given for the elementary pupils who score the highest in a written mathematics quiz—usually an excerpt from a SAT preparation manual of which there are many on sale at all book stores.

Industrial Arts

The Industrial arts show is often one of the highlights of the year that the local public looks forward to attending each year. Held either in the evening or on a Saturday, students display their projects in wood, metal, electricity, and graphic arts and are on hand to explain to any interested viewer how he went about making the project.

Often the articles are for sale, and after a student has paid the school for the material he used, he is permitted to keep the rest of the money. This procedure encourages many students to put their best efforts into their work and to use their time wisely to produce as many projects as possible during the year.

Some of the larger items such as cabinets, tables, dressers and divans sell for several hundred dollars and, if they are well made, are in great demand.

In the graphic arts department orders are taken for business and personal stationery, business cards, circulars, and other forms of printed matter. Again, the student who receives the order retains the profit after reimbursing the school for the materials.

Metal objects from the metal shop—ornate copper wall ornaments, candlesticks, napkin rings, and jewelry are also on display and many are on sale by their makers.

Occasionally, local merchants raise an objection to the sale of furniture, bric-a-brac, jewelry, printed matter, and other articles produced by the industrial arts department, claiming that these sales cut into their own profits. However, since the industrial arts show is held only once a year, in most communities the merchants, although not pleased with the competition, hold back from making any complaints.

Art Department

Hallowe'en Decorating Contest. A very popular extracurricular activity of the art department, widespread in popularity throughout the country, is the hallowe'en window decorating contest. Store windows along "Main Street" are assigned to various students from the art club who design and execute a typical hallowe'en scene on the glass window using tempera paints which can be easily removed when the holiday has passed.

These windows are judged by local artists and prizes are awarded.

Art Show. Another popular activity produced by the high school art club is the art show. Often it is held along the main street of town. Paintings, works of sculpture, examples of hobbies and crafts are displayed along the sidewalks with students standing by to answer questions about their work. If the town or city has an indoor mall, the show probably will be held in its main corridors. Sometimes the art show is held at the school, either in the gymnasium or in the art rooms.

Foreign Language

The Foreign Language Banquet is a favorite project of many foreign language departments. These banquets are attended by the students taking a foreign language, their parents, and invited guests from the school and town.

Each table features a different language, and the food (cooked by members of the home economics department) is typical of the type of cuisine served in that country.

After the meal is concluded, students often will present a program which consists of dances and songs from each of the represented countries.

Physical Education Department

In addition to regularly scheduled interclass evening games held in the gymnasium, many heads of the physical education department put on gymnastic exhibits for the general public. Tumbling, mat work, parallel bars, and rings are featured. Students in the regular gym classes practice for this event weeks in advance, and any student who wishes to may take part.

R.O.T.C. Drill Teams. Although not an actual part of the physical education department, the R.O.T.C. units (Reserve Officer's Training Corps) are closely affiliated with physical education. At least once a year the students who have signed up for R.O.T.C. stage a parade and review which consists of open and closed drill, presenting arms and other military maneuvers.

The public is generally invited to attend, and usually present are officers from the state units to inspect and grade the work of the students.

SCHOOL-WIDE HIGH SCHOOL EXTRACURRICULAR ACTIVITIES

In addition to those clubs and activities sponsored by the different subject matter departments, a high school also has a number of school-wide organizations which are open to all students, or open to only those students who are eligible. The extracurricular activities listed below are common to most high schools throughout the nation.

Key Club. Sponsored by the local Kiwanis Club, key club members represent the leaders of the schools, those who have made a name for themselves because of high scholarship, leadership, and community service. Membership is by invitation and is open to both boys and girls.

National Honor Society. Members of the National Honor Society are selected because of their consistently high grades.

Student Government. Some form of student government has been a part of the high school scene since just after World War I. At that time the United States had, for the first time, become a world power; nationalism was high throughout the land, and a new meaning to democracy was beginning to emerge.

School officials translated this new form of democracy into their curriculum by conceiving the idea of a student government—a president, vice president, and elected representatives from each homeroom.

Actually very little decision-making was given to this legislative body. Full authority was retained by the administrators because they believed that minors of high school age were incapable of governing themselves.

Instead, superficial problems were turned over to the students by school officials in an attempt to give some relevance to their existence as a governing body. Such minor decision-making as where the arbor day tree should be planted, how the gymnasium should be decorated for the annual spring hop, or who should be picked to raise the American flag each morning on the flagpole in front of the school are examples of the type of decision-making left to the student council.

As time went on and students became more aware of their rights, and more rights were given to them by Supreme Court decisions, school officials found themselves ceding more and more authority to the student body.

Today, in many schools, this governing body enacts rules and regulations for the conduct of students and draws up the type of punishment for those who disobey them. Often a student "court" is a part of the plan and delinquent students' cases are heard by the court and sentence passed.

More and more high schools are selecting a member of the student government body to represent the students on the board of education. Legally this representative has no vote, but board members listen seriously to what he has to say and often vote in support of his requests.

At first school officials feared the consequences of placing so much authority in the hands of students, but as time passed and many of the problems formerly falling upon their shoulders were being solved by the student government, the administration found no further cause for concern.

School Dances and Proms. The student government as part of its fund raising activities, sponsors several dances throughout the school year. Normally these dances are held in the gymnasium, but occasionally, for special events such as the junior and senior prom, the events may be held in one of the larger more luxurious restaurants in the neighborhood.

Cheerleaders and Flag Twirlers. Of all the activities open to girls, becoming a member of the cheerleaders or flagtwirlers is often the most important thing that could happen to them. Competition is fierce. Girls begin practicing when they are six and seven years old, and look forward to the day when they will be able to try out for the team and, hopefully, be selected.

In most schools tryouts are held every year, and acceptance one year does not guarantee renewal for the next. Ornate uniforms and spectacular pom-poms are issued to the cheerleaders; uniforms, batons, and flags to the twirlers. A girl who is a member of either of these teams is looked up to by her peers.

Some schools permit boys to try out for cheerleading and twirling.

Band. No school that fields a football team can be without a band! A good part of the strong school spirit generated during a football game between two rival schools is produced by the timely playing from the band.

Many bands throughout the country become so proficient that they are invited to participate in events of national importance—presidential inaugurations, football bowl games, Fourth of July celebrations, and special event parades in large cities.

These bands work feverishly throughout the year to raise the necessary funds to pay for their transportation and hotel expenses. Selling candy, sponsoring car washes, collecting at supermarket entrances are ways these funds are raised.

And the host city and football team receive free entertainment.

Choir and Chorus. Each year the band and choir combined put on several programs, one at Christmas and another later in the year. They are open to the public free of charge. Some choirs and choruses also perform at nursing homes and hospitals, particularly before the Christmas season.

Awards Assembly and Graduation. Prior to graduation many schools schedule an awards assembly during which time seniors are presented with scholarships, trophies, prizes, and other awards. Formerly these prizes were given out during graduation exercises, but because of the length of time consumed, this portion of graduation exercises has been moved to a prior time in many schools.

Graduation exercises are held in many different types of locations — theaters, arenas, out-of-doors, in the school gymnasium. Speeches are given and diplomas are handed out.

The most effective graduation exercises are those during which the administration, teachers and outside speakers are kept to a minimum and the graduation is student-oriented.

Back-to-School-Night. During American Education week many schools celebrate the occasion by holding a back-to-school-night. Parents follow their son's or daughter's schedule and have the opportunity to meet with each teacher who gives the parents a brief synopsis of the objectives of the course. No personal problems are discussed, but parents may make appointments to meet with the teacher at a later date.

Pep Rallies and Pregame Bonfires. If permission has been obtained from the local fire department and if the school has a piece of vacant land which is suitable, many boards of education permit prefootball game bonfires. At these events the cheerleaders and twirlers perform, the football squad is introduced and given an ovation, speeches are made by the coach and assistant coaches, and those student body members and teaching staff who have attended cheer, hoot, holler, and have a great time.

The pep rally is a close cousin of the pregame bonfire. Usually it is held in the gymnasium the last period of the day before an important game, and the same type of program is presented—cheerleaders and cheers from the student body, the introduction of the squad, speeches from the coaches and principal, and music from the school's marching band.

National Book Week. The school media center celebrates National Book Week by holding a book fair. Book fairs take on many versions—a display of newly purchased books; storytelling hours, sponsored and run by Library Club students for elementary age children; and talks by local authors.

Field Trips. Although field trips are usually an outgrowth of the curriculum of a subject department, many schools also run school-wide field trips. The most prevalent type is the Senior trip, often associated with the senior prom and graduation. Washington, D.C., Niagara Falls, and Williamsburg are favorite places to visit for schools on the East Coast. Disneyland attracts schools from the West; Disney World, Epcot, and Sea World for those in South.

Occasionally a school will sponsor trips abroad during the summer months, especially for students who wish to expand their knowledge of a foreign language.

Assemblies. Many schools still schedule an occasional assembly, not on a regular basis as the schools of the past did, but as the need and occasion arises. Because most auditoriums are not large enough to house the entire student body at one sitting, assemblies are repeated a sufficient number of times to accommodate all students, or only those students who are interested in seeing the assembly are invited.

Educational as well as entertaining programs are the bill of fare. Popular rock groups, talks by former addicts, magicians, jugglers, scientists, and hypnotists are the type of programs enjoyed the most by today's teenagers.

Parents should examine the extracurricular program of their high school carefully because, next to the regular curriculum, this part of school life is next in importance. A growing, dynamic school will have a wide variety of extracurricular activities, well-attended by its student body, and thoroughly endorsed and supported by its faculty.

Evaluation

Rate each of the following statements by placing an x beneath the number which best describes the conditions in your community's school. Then draw a continuous line through the x's to form a graph.

1   2   3   4   5

- A comprehensive, flexible extracurricular program is introduced in the upper grades of elementary school or in the middle school.
- The extracurricular program in the upper grades of the elementary school or in the middle school is functioning with good results.
- The staff of the elementary school or middle school regularly reviews the effectiveness of its extracurricular program and makes necessary changes.
- Subject departments in the high school offer the following clubs: (Score high if a club is offered; low, if not offered.)

  Drama Club

  School newspaper

  School magazine

  Science fairs

  Astronomy night observations or visits to planetariums

  Fashion shows featuring clothing made by students

  Mathematics contests

  Industrial arts show and sales

  Hallowe'en decorating contests

  Art shows

  Foreign language banquets

  Gymnastic Exhibitions

  R.O.T.C. parades and drill teams

  Key Club

  National Honor Society

  Student government

  Student court

  School dances and proms

  Cheerleaders

  Flag twirlers (Baton twirlers)

  Band

  Choir

  Awards assembly

  Graduation exercises conducted mainly by the graduates

  Back-to-school-night

  Pep rallies, (bon fires, if permitted)

  National Book Week

  Field trips

  Assemblies

  Other extra curricular programs not included above

Chapter Eleven

THE ADMINISTRATION

"Why does this school system need a superintendent of schools, two assistant superintendents, five principals, and six assistant principals? It's my understanding that the total pupil population of the district has been decreasing each year for the past five years, from about three thousand two hundred to two thousand seven hundred, and yet we actually *added* one administrator during that time."

Questions like this one are brought up by citizenry at board of education meetings across the country time and time again. And often boards are hard-pressed to come up with a convincing answer because *many school districts do have more administrators than are needed to do an efficient job.*

The superintendent of schools, the chief administrator of the district, feels most secure when he is surrounded by a large contingent of aides—assistant superintendents, curriculum advisors, and coordinators for various agencies. Boards of education, which are composed of lay people, often do not understand the workings of a school, particularly the administrative branch. Consequently, when the superintendent requests an additional staff member for his office, most boards are hard pressed not to honor the request.

Most public indignation concerning a top-heavy administrative staff occurs at budget time, particularly when school taxes in the district have been rising each year and the total pupil population has been declining. In the interim, teachers may have been laid off, sports programs cut, transportation routes reduced—but the administrative staff remains intact.

When asked for an explanation, the board will in all likelihood turn to the superintendent. He will explain that now, at last, with a diminishing student population, his staff will have the time to face the real issues, such as curriculum revision, textbook revision, and teacher evaluation, which just had to sit on the shelf until now because of the low ratio of administrators to student population which formerly existed. And how can an uninformed citizen dispute such a statement? He can't. He takes his seat, probably more confused than ever.

There are no simple formulae to determine the number of administrators that a district needs in order to do an efficient job of directing and maintaining a school district. Conditions vary within districts across the country. An inner city school with overwhelming discipline and drug problems probably will need more administrators than a suburban district where 90 or more percent of its students intend to go on to college.

Other factors also play an important part in assessing the numerical number of administrators needed by a district. A school system which has a strong guidance department in all its schools can reduce the number of assistant principals needed because guidance counselors can assume many of the duties of the assistant principal.

Often, to camouflage the number of administrators, a board of education will assign a different name to the position: Coordinator of Bus Transportation, Supervisor of Maintenance, Director of Buildings and Grounds, or Chief Financial Officer instead of Assistant Superintendent in Charge of Transportation, Assistant Superintendent in Charge of Maintenance and Repair, Assistant Superintendent of Buildings and Grounds, or Assistant Superintendent of Finance.

The real test is to compare salaries. If these offices are drawing the same or nearly equal salaries to those of the assistant superintendents, then it can be assumed that their title has been changed to fool the public.

The public has a right to know if its tax dollars are being spent to the best advantage. The real test in any public school system is how effective the educational program is, whether it is serving the needs of *all* its pupils. If the administration can justify the number of assistant superintendents, principals, assistant principals it has placed on its payroll, then the public has no right to criticize.

But most taxpayers have no standard by which to judge the accuracy or authenticity of whatever explication its administrators have provided in defense of its position. Needed is a job description of each of these offices. Therefore, the following pages will be deal with the duties and responsibilities of the superintendent, assistant superintendents, principals, assistant principals and other administrators who go by various titles depending upon the school system.

The Superintendent. The superintendent serves as the chief school administrator and the liaison between the board of education and the entire personnel of the school system. In some districts, the board secretary or chief fiscal administrator may be directly responsible to the board of education and not to the superintendent.

Each board of education should adopt a chart showing the chain of command, and this chart should be available to the public. Examination of the chain of command is important to anyone who is in the process of evaluating the administration.

Today, most superintendents of schools have earned a doctorate of education degree. However, it should be pointed out that possession of such a degree does not in itself guarantee that the individual is well qualified for the position. I have known a number of superintendents who do not have such a degree and outperform many who do.

There are certain qualities a superintendent must possess if he wishes to succeed in his profession. At the top of the list is the ability to lead others. Leadership is a term that encompasses a number of subordinate traits. Certainly the type of leadership necessary in an army officer differs considerably from that required in a school executive. The school superintendent must exhibit at all times a thorough knowledge of educational philosophies and current trends in the profession. He must be able to steer his staff in the direction he wishes the school system to move. He must invoke the confidence of his staff in the decisions he makes. And, probably most important of all, he must at all times be in good standing with his board of education.

In a large school system the superintendent of schools will allocate many of his responsibilities to his assistants, much as the President of the United States allocates his responsibilities to his cabinet. Furthermore, like the President, the superintendent must be "on top" of all decisions and policy-making promulgated by his subordinates.

He does this by frequent staff meetings. At these meetings he receives oral reports from his subordinates as to their progress on previously-assigned problems. Or the superintendent may request written reports on a regular basis.

Coordinating the information he receives from these varied sources constitutes another phase of leadership ability. This requires much thought and planning on the superintendent's part. The results must consummate in action that moves the school system forward or resolves some previous problem.

Information gained without action taken is a futile and time-consuming "game" that some superintendents play with their subordinates, usually not for long, however. More than one superintendent has been faced with a vote of "no confidence" from the teaching staff or his administrative subordinates because he played the "information received, information noted" game which resulted in a thick file carefully put away for future reference.

And such "no confidence" votes by a teachers' organization are not to be taken lightly by any superintendent who values his position and wishes to remain in his post. The media are quick to seize upon such news stories, and once they do, the public will become involved and the board of education will be inundated with questions and complaints. Sides will be taken within the community and often a rift occurs that takes a long time to heal.

Many boards, to relieve the problem, find no choice but to dismiss the superintendent. If he is under tenure, and will not leave voluntarily, many boards of education have resorted to "buying out" the superintendent by offering him a large enough sum of money to leave and seek another post.

In addition to good leadership qualities, there are other traits which a superintendent must have. Briefly these include a pleasing personality, ability to get along with others, the stamina needed to take the "hard knocks" inherent to his office, the ability to organize, the ability to think creatively, a pleasing manner and excellence in addressing large groups of people, and that innate quality some people have to be able to foresee which plans will work and which will not.

The superintendent's office, with the assistance of any assistant superintendents, is responsible for the following major areas of school management:

The Hiring and Firing of Teachers. The Evaluation of All Personnel. Although the laws in most states relegates the authority to hire and fire personnel only to the boards of education, most boards rubber stamp the recommendation of their superintendent.

Nowadays, in order to dismiss a teacher or other employee who is not under tenure, the administration must make repeated observations of the individual's work and keep detailed evaluative documents, one copy of which goes to the employee. In addition, if the work is unsatisfactory, the administrator in charge of personnel must have a conference with the employee after each unsatisfactory evaluation.

Furthermore, it is in the best interest of the school system if more than one administrator evaluates the employee and also finds the work unsatisfactory. Usually, when a teacher's work is in question, the superintendent, the assistant superintendent, the principal and vice principal of the school, and the department head of the high school subject area will all observe the teacher in the classroom.

One assistant superintendent is usually responsible for hiring new teachers. After he has narrowed the field to two or three candidates, he will usually invite the superintendent to sit in for the final decision making. The final candidate will be recommended to the board of education.

Providing Substitute Teachers. A large school system has need of dozens of substitute teachers each day school is in session. The substitute list is made up of retired teachers who wish to supplement their income, housewives who were former teachers and whose children are now of school-age, and recent graduates from colleges who have not yet found a permanent teaching position.

An employee of the board of education is designated as the one responsible for filling all teacher absences each day. A teacher must call in to this individual at least several hours before the opening of school, anywhere from five-thirty to seven o'clock in the morning.

Selecting and Purchasing Textbooks and Supplies. Because this is, for the most part, a seasonal job, it is usually assigned in conjunction with other duties. Actually the selection of the texts is a function of the teachers who will use them, in conjunction with the department head in the high school, and the curriculum coordinator in the elementary school.

Preparing the Annual Budget. This is a task which requires the input from many sources—teachers, department heads, principals, head janitors, cafeteria managers, athletic directors, maintenance personnel, assistant superintendent in charge of transportation and a host of other employees. All of this information must be compiled and studied. If any of the requests appear to be excessive, then conferences with the individuals making the requests must be set up and a compromise worked out.

When all of the figures have been decided upon, they must then be aggregated and placed in the proper portion of the tentative budget.

Pupil Transportation. In many districts, particularly those in suburbia and in the sparsely populated areas of the country, getting thousands of students to school is a momentous task. First, bus routes must be established. To accomplish this every student must be pinpointed on a map of the area. A route is then created with no more students assigned than the maximum capacity of the bus.

A sufficient number of bus drivers must then be hired. Their backgrounds must be checked thoroughly, including their driving record and any arrests for criminal activity. Substitute drivers must also be hired.

Buses must be maintained and checked periodically for any possible defects. New buses need to be purchased after about ten years of use. A safe storage area during the summer months is a necessity, particularly in areas where the number of cases of vandalism is high.

In addition all buses must be inspected in most states at least once a year. Insurance policies must be obtained.

Planning and Building New Schoolhouses. In rapidly growing communities new schoolhouses are constantly on the drawing boards. That branch of the administrative staff responsible for providing sufficient classrooms must be cognizant of the changing growth patterns of the district and, therefore, planning for new schoolhouses at least four to five years in advance.

One of the jobs of the school-planning staff is to purchase the necessary land for these new schoolhouses and to do it quietly before land developers become aware of the plans and buy up these tracts on speculation.

Furnishing New Schoolhouses. Usually the same department that plans the new schoolhouses also furnishes them. More on this topic can be found by referring to Chapter Three, Equipment.

Submitting Federal and State Reports. No one in the public domain can appreciate the reams of paper work that school officials are now required to turn in to state and federal agencies. To discuss each of these forms would be futile, because they change with each new federal and state program and with each new bill that is passed requiring more facts and figures to be filed in state and federal archives or to become the basis for some legislator's speech.

Preparing Applications for Special State and Federal Grants. Today the school that can come up with the most innovative educational program, and that has the ability to write it up in an appealing, provocative manner, comes home with the federal and state special grant monies.

Setting up Classes for Atypical Students. Providing classes for the atypical student has, during the last twenty years, been legislated by every state in the country. Prior to World War II, students with special needs and special problems were either mainstreamed with their classmates, or placed on home instruction. Now special classes are held for the deaf, the educable mentally retarded, the trainable mentally retarded, the blind, the exceptional child, the physically handicapped, and for non-English speaking students.

Reporting to the Board of Education. It is usually the superintendent of schools who maintains a liaison with the board of education. He attends all their regular and special meetings, and at most of them it is his agenda that requires the greatest amount of time and attention from the board. He supplies them with the information they, as individuals and as a body, must be cognizant of when dealing with the public. And he brings his list of requests, because only the board can authorize the expenditure of money, the hiring and firing of personnel, the adoption of a curriculum, the building of a new schoolhouse, or the acquisition of new or additional supplies and equipment.

Managing the School Cafeterias. The assistant superintendent in charge of cafeterias must, as part of his duties, furnish each cafeteria with sufficient foodstuffs, hire personnel to man the kitchens, arrange for the removal of trash and garbage, and prepare the weekly menus.

Managing the Fiscal Affairs of the Board of Education. This branch of school management is headed by a business manager or board of education secretary who may or may not be directly responsible to the superintendent. His responsibilities include keeping the books, recording the minutes of all board meetings, issuing purchase orders, purchasing insurance policies, and keeping an inventory of all properties owned by the board of education.

The Assistant Superintendents. In larger school systems the job of the superintendent is made easier by supplying him with assistants. How he makes use of these assistants is a matter of individual preference. The most common method is to assign each assistant certain duties: Assistant superintendent in charge of curriculum, Assistant Superintendent in Charge of Supplies and Equipment, Assistant Superintendent in Charge of Transportation, Assistant Superintendent in Charge of Personnel, and so forth, as listed above under "superintendent," thus dividing up all of the principal areas of school management.

In a large school system the administrative staff is usually housed in a building separate from any classrooms. Often it is a converted school which, because of its age, would be too costly to renovate for use as classrooms but lends itself structurally as an office building. Here are housed the superintendent, all assistant superintendents, secretaries, and clerks.

School Principals and Vice Principals. The principal is the chief executive of a school; he is responsible to the superintendent for maintaining and improving the educational climate of the building to which he has been assigned. The vice principal is his assistant and is usually assigned to the task of maintaining student control.

Maintaining and improving the educational climate of a school is a demanding job. Following are the main elements of his duties:

1. *To assist teachers in solving any problems which they are unable to resolve by themselves.* In a typical day a teacher may come to him because the temperature in the classroom is so warm pupils cannot concentrate; because the movie projector is broken; because one of the students appears to have been the victim of child abuse; because Jimmy is disobedient and refuses to do his work; because a parent has entered the classroom uninvited and is carrying on in front of the class, and refuses to leave; because the janitor has not been cleaning the classroom and blackboard satisfactorily over a period of many days; because Susan's lunch money was stolen. The list is endless.

2. *To evaluate the staff and other employees and to work with those who need improvement.* Periodic evaluations of the teachers is an important part of the principal and vice principal's job. Evaluative reports, after being discussed with the teacher, are sent to the superintendent's office.

3. *Conferring with Parents.* In a single school day, the principal will find that a number of parents wish to speak with him about some problem, usually one relating to the behavior or achievement of their son or daughter. Such complaints usually must be followed through with a teacher conference and a subsequent final meeting with the parent.

In addition to meeting with parents, the principal or vice principal will have scheduled meetings with civic leaders, salesmen, the police chief, the fire captain, reporters, the superintendent of schools, and occasionally with members of the board of education, to name just a few.

4. *To work with teachers in curriculum revision.* This is a constant, ongoing phase of his work and an extremely important one. In the elementary school he will divide his faculty into several groups, each studying a different level of the curriculum. Each will meet at a separate time so that the principal or vice principal can be in attendance.

For curriculum revision the high school principal will work through his department heads, who in turn, will work through the teachers in their department. The principal may sit in on these and all curriculum meetings, or he may delegate some portion of this duty to an assistant principal.

5. *To conduct frequent teachers' meetings, at which time various problems of concern to the entire faculty are discussed.* Some principals space their teachers' meetings at regular intervals—every week or every two weeks, for instance. Others call a meeting only after sufficient topics for discussions have arisen to require a meeting.

Here are some typical problems discussed at teachers' meetings:

Revising the format of the report card.

Streamlining the system of recording grades on a master sheet and getting these grades to the homeroom teacher who then records them on the student's report card.

Resolving the problem of students roaming the hallways after dismissal.

Overcrowded lunch periods which results in some students not having time to eat after going through the serving lines.

Students parking in teachers' assigned parking spaces.

Noise from the band rehearsing outside when other classes are in session.

Attendance-taking techniques.

Students dismissed early to attend field trips, intramural sports events, and band and play practice.

Too many students called to the office and to guidance during class time.

6. *To take charge of student scheduling, class assignments, teacher assignments and room assignments.* Before the opening of each school year, the high school principal, with the assistance of his subordinates, decides the number of sections that will be needed for each subject, which rooms these sections will meet in, which teacher will be assigned, and which periods of the day they will meet. When these data have been decided upon and fed into the computer, then each student's schedule for the coming year can be determined.

Department Heads. Most high schools appoint a master teacher to serve as department head. His duties vary from school to school, but in general he is responsible for curriculum development, teacher evaluation, textbook selection, inventory-keeping within his department, liaison with other departments and the administration, and assistance in selecting new teachers.

Department heads may be required to teach anywhere from four classes to none at all, depending on the size of the school and the extent of his department head duties. Besides being relieved of a normal day's teaching load, he may receive extra compensation above his teacher's salary. He may also be placed on a twelve-month contract and usually is considered as part of the administration.

Other Administrative Personnel. Other personnel, not part of the educational staff of the school system, include the Chief of Transportation, Cafeteria Managers, the Chief Medical Inspector, the Board of Education Fiscal Administrator, Head of Grounds and Maintenance, and Head of Security.

Evaluation

Rate each of the following statements by placing an x beneath the number which best describes the conditions in your community's high school. Then connect all the x's with a continuous line to form a graph.

1 2 3 4 5

- Your school district has an adequate number of administrators and no more.
- Your school district, if losing pupil enrollment, decreases the number of administrators accordingly.
- Your school district has a chart indicating the chain of command and this chart is available to the public.
- Your superintendent of schools has exhibited leadership qualities in his dealings with the board of education, his staff, and the public.
- Neither your superintendent nor any of his assistants has ever been given a "no confidence" vote by his staff.
- Your superintendent of schools, or his designated assistant, adequately performs his duties to:

    Hire and fire teachers.

    Provide an adequate number of good substitute teachers.

    Provide all students with up-to-date texts.

    Provide a safe, efficient transportation system for students.

    Plan and build sufficient school-houses so no classes are ever on double session or overcrowded.

    Brings in federal and state grants for innovative educational programs.

    Provides well-run cafeterias that serve nutritious food at a reasonable cost.

    Manages the board's fiscal affairs so that the budget is never over-spent.

    Issues purchase orders for all purchases.

- The principals of all schools perform their task adequately.
- Department heads in the high school perform their tasks adequately.

Chapter Twelve

DISCIPLINE

In previous chapters we have talked about teacher-control within the classroom. This chapter will deal with the kind of climate that should prevail throughout the school. Obviously, the two are interrelated. It is difficult for a teacher to maintain order within the classroom if students are permitted to run wild in the remainder of the building. And conversely, there is, to a lesser degree, a bearing on school control when a classroom is in disorder; more so when several classrooms have lost control.

Recently, when a group of parents was questioned about concerns they had for their child's school, over 80 percent listed school discipline first. The problem is nationwide.

Before we can discuss the causes and possible cures, we must first understand what is meant by "a breakdown in discipline" and what constitutes a favorable climate for learning.

A hundred years ago students sat rigidly at their desks, raised their hands and were called upon before speaking, stood up each time they recited, left the room in single file with no talking permitted. They lined up quietly in the hall and a few at a time were permitted to enter the boys' or girls' room, or to get a drink at the fountain. Our forefathers considered this type of behavior appropriate for learning.

Educators and psychologists of today believe that with such strict rules of conduct, children do not learn as effectively as they do when a degree of freedom is permitted. Children, they believe, must be somewhat uninhibited in their behavior or their process of creative thinking can be stifled.

Elementary School Discipline. Because children do not move about the building as extensively as they do in the middle school and high school, the potential for a breakdown in discipline is not as great. Many of the school buildings now being constructed have toilet facilities and drinking fountains included as part of each classroom, and therefore, except for lunch break and recess, no pupil needs to leave the classroom until dismissal.

175

In schools where there are only centrally located toilet facilities, the classroom teacher takes the class several times a day and supervises the operation from the time the pupils leave the room until they return.

Lunchroom supervision is more difficult. In elementary schools with a small enrollment, one lunch period usually suffices. In larger schools as many as two or three may be necessary. The administration must schedule these lunch periods so that each teacher gets a duty-free lunch for himself, and yet a sufficient number of teachers are on duty to monitor the lunch period.

In schools where special teachers, such as physical education, art, and music, take over a teacher's class, the classroom teachers can then be assigned to lunch duty. In schools where the classroom teacher is not freed by the visitation of special teachers, or where negotiations between the board of education and the teachers' union have resulted in a duty-free lunch period for *all* teachers, special lunchroom supervisors are hired.

A relative of mine took such a position a few years ago. After a few weeks on the job she quit. When I asked her why, she replied, "I just couldn't take it any more. The children eat like pigs. They throw their food on the floor. They throw it at one another. When I tell them to pick it up, they say to me, 'You pick it up. That's what you're hired for.' I complained to the principal. He told me if I couldn't control the kids then I wasn't the one for the job. So I quit."

I learned later that three other supervisors had quit, one after the other, and they all gave the same reason. The kids acted like slobs. The principal wanted no part of the problem.

Equally difficult to control are assemblies. Most programs are conducted in a darkened auditorium, making supervision virtually impossible. Pupils in the upper grades come armed with rubber bands and spitballs. Or they talk in loud voices throughout the program. Or they may annoy the child sitting in front of them. Identification of the culprits is extremely difficult. The most a teacher can do if she is able to pick out the offender is remove the child from the auditorium and send him to the office.

As a result of the difficulties of conducting assembly programs, many elementary schools have done away with them. Auditoriums that cost hundreds of thousands of dollars to build sit empty. Valuable educational programs can no longer be presented.

On the other hand, there are many elementary schools where the faculty is still in control. The secret of their success is found in one fundamental principle of mass pupil control: the first time an incident occurs, the program is stopped and the students returned to their classroom. Or, if only a few students are responsible for the interruption, the program is halted, the lights are turned on, and the students identified; they are removed from the room and their parents notified. If this process is repeated each time a disturbance occurs, the student body will soon acclimate itself to the rules and act accordingly.

Another area of the elementary school which has the potential for causing disciplinary problems is the playground. Here children in the lower grades are usually permitted to organize their own individual play activities. Hopscotch, rope jumping, tag, hide-and-go-seek, and various ball games are encouraged by the teacher.

But there are always a few children who do not join in any of these activities, and they are the ones who are potential troublemakers. They will push and shove other children, get into fights, grab jumping ropes away from the players and run away with them, and taunt and tease anyone with whom they come in contact. These children can cause serious problems for a teacher if their antics are not stopped. As time goes on, other children will drop out of the organized activities and join them, and before long the entire group will be out of control.

In the middle and upper grades organized games are the usual activity and control is more easily maintained. At this age, boys and girls are avidly sports-minded, and the teacher who prepares for the playground period will have no difficulties maintaining discipline.

Discipline at the High School Level. One educator once remarked that "teenagers are inherent mischief-makers." There may be some truth in his statement. Teenagers are at that stage in life when they find satisfaction in testing adults and, if they find a weakness there, to exploit it.

If this be so, then the wise school administrator makes certain that the rules and regulations he promulgates are, first of all fair and just, and second, that they are enforced at all times with no exceptions.

It should be noted, and emphasized, that running a tight ship in the modern high school is no easy task. Many ills of our modern-day society have spilled over into our schools; hundreds of high schools, particularly those in the inner cities, are time bombs waiting to go off.

To understand the problems facing today's high school principal and his staff, let's take a look at the type of disciplinary problems they face. We'll start with the least severe and work toward the acute.

1. *Running in the Halls.* While this may not seem to be of any conse-

quence, serious accidents can result when hundreds of students are changing classes and a few students decide to chase one another, either in jest or in anger. Or when a few students are in a hurry to get to their next class, or to meet their girlfriends at a prearranged time and place. Anyone who gets in their way can be thrown to the floor or knocked against a locker.

2. *Shouting.* This is another minor infraction of the rules in many schools. Some students are naturally "loudmouthed." Male students have the belief that being loud is being manly. While shouting in itself cannot cause harm to others, it could result in serious consequences in case an emergency should develop and someone in authority must give directions.

3. *Looking into Classrooms in Session.* Students who are out of their classes with a boys' or girls' room pass often make it a habit to take the long way back so they can peer into classrooms to see what their boy friends or girl friends are doing. If they can catch their attention and gesture to them, so much the better. Some are even so bold as to enter the room to talk to their friend.

4. *Banging on Lockers.* Teenagers today apparently love noise in any form. One habit a number of students have developed nationwide, it seems, is walking down the hall while pounding on every locker, or running a pencil, coin or other object from locker to locker.

5. *Setting Off Fire Alarms.* Some students do this to get a break from class, particularly if they are about to be given a test. Others just like the excitement of causing everyone to leave the building. Schools where the fire system is tied to the police department or the fire house have a particular problem with false alarms.

6. *Truancy.* Habitual absence from school is a real problem in many high schools. Truants are usually boys and girls who have lost all interest in an education and are waiting for their sixteenth birthday so they can drop out of school legally. Rounding up these truants from the city's street corners becomes a daily function of the truant officer; day after day he brings in the same students who spend the remaining few hours disrupting their classes in the hope they may be suspended, thus giving them a few days or a week during which time the truant officer can't bother them.

7. *Fighting.* Fighting usually takes place outside on school grounds after school because it has been prearranged by the participants. Word spreads quickly as to the time and place, and huge crowds of students

gather to witness the confrontation. Occasionally, however, a spontaneous fight will erupt in the halls between class periods, and again crowds will gather to watch it until some teacher or administrators breaks it up.

8. *Drag Racing.* Most suburban high schools have extensive on-site roadways and parking areas, and these are a natural attraction for the drag-race enthusiasts. The race is usually arranged ahead of time and often bets are placed on the outcome.

Serious injury and even death have resulted from these races, injuries to the participants and to the many bystanders who congregate along the path of the race. Often parked cars are sideswiped and in some cases the school district has been found liable.

9. *Smoking.* Restricting cigarette smoking by students has been a problem for many years, but it is one that has been worsening recently as students become more aggressive and assertive in their demands. Some schools have solved the problem to some extent by designating certain smoking areas where students may go during lunch hour and at other times when they are not in class.

But other schools have felt that to permit smoking on school grounds and at the same time to teach the evils of alcohol and tobacco in health classes is contradictive and hypocritical. But these schools are then faced with a difficult time attempting to enforce the restrictions.

Go into any one of them and you will find that the boys' and girls' rooms are so clouded with cigarette smoke that one cannot see across the room. Nonsmokers and their parents complain to authorities about the health hazards their children are subjected to when they use these rooms.

10. *Vandalism.* I know of several newly opened high schools whose interiors have been completely demolished by student vandals within a few months of opening. Partitions in the boys' and girls' rooms have been ripped from the walls. Sinks and toilets pulled loose. Walls in the halls covered with graffiti. Cafeteria tables and chairs twisted out of shape so they were no longer serviceable. Blackboards in classrooms cracked and pulled from the walls. Lighting fixtures hanging precariously from the ceiling. The list of damage goes on and on.

Unfortunately there is a certain element of today's youth who gain pleasure from destroying things.

11. *Alcohol Abuse.* Although most states in the country have raised the legal drinking age to twenty-one, high school students apparently find no problem in purchasing all the liquor they want. The number of teenage alcoholics in this country has reached alarming proportions.

Beer parties for children as young as ten and twelve have been broken up by police in cities across the country.

The problem carries over into the schools. Many times during the school year parents must be called to come to school and pick up their son or daughter who is too drunk to drive. Beer and other alcoholic beverages are smuggled into school and hidden in lockers where they are consumed between class periods.

12. *Thefts.* Although stealing has always been a problem in schools, today it has taken on a new twist. Perhaps extortion would be a better term to use than theft. Gangs of youth prey on younger students and threaten their safety unless they "contribute" money on a regular basis. Many of these students are forced to go without lunch because they must give up their lunch money every day.

School property is also stolen — video cameras, computers, typewriters, record players, video cassettes, movie projectors, microscopes, and other items which can be easily pawned are smuggled out of the building.

Student lockers are pried open and valuables removed. In isolated areas of the building, students may be waylaid and their wallets or pocketbooks forcefully taken from them.

Many schools have hired security patrols to cover the hallways and foyers to protect students from these muggings, but even the best of patrols cannot be in all places at one time.

13. *Sex.* We are living in an age when sexual behavior is often openly expressed and uninhibited. Certain segments of the adolescent population, more than any other group, express themselves freely whether they are at home, parked somewhere in an automobile, or in school.

"Necking" is done openly in many schools — while walking down the halls, in the classroom, in the back of an empty auditorium, or after school somewhere about the campus. Sexual acts are more discreet, but they, too, unfortunately, are a part of the American high school scene.

14. *Drugs.* It seems that high school officials barely become acclimated to the ramifications of one type of drug being used by students when another appears on the scene. Over the last twenty or thirty years scores of different narcotics have been "the in thing" with youth, from LSD to angel dust, to "grass," to crack, to inhalants of many kinds, to cough medicines. If any substance has the ability to bring on a "high," children will learn about it and experiment with it.

No one needs to be told how serious the drug problem is among the youth of this nation. Every day the health and safety of thousands of teenagers is being affected. And every day another young boy or girl is being killed by this scourge, as exemplified by this recent newspaper release:

INHALANTS CAUSE OF TEEN'S DEATH

Medical and law enforcement officials are reaching out to the youth of St. Johns County in an effort to bring home the dangers of sniffing household products after the death of a high school teenager who, his friends stated, had inhaled three bottles of correction fluid.

Inhalants, along with all the other substance abuse topics, have been a part of the drug awareness curriculum in the county's schools, but the sheriff's office now plans to inaugurate a separate program for the Deputy Youth Reserve Officers who are stationed at the county high schools to put into effect.

"Unfortunately, all the emphasis in the past four or five years has been placed on marijuana and cocaine," said Captain Robert Porter. "Inhalants just got lost in the flood of concentration on crack."

Prohibiting the bringing of drugs to school has been a problem that school officials have never totally solved. Various decisions by the Supreme Court giving minors the rights of adults have made the problem more difficult to solve. Back in the days when students could be searched, when every locker in a school could, without warning, be inspected, then school officials could keep a school "clean" of drugs and alcohol.

Today the drug peddlers can make their sales on school property, and school officials have a difficult time preventing it from taking place. Some schools have tried placing police at all entrances, but this action did little more than to force the pushers from the building to the street outside.

New Jersey has recently passed a law that makes the penalty for selling drugs within a designated school zone far more severe than if sold at other locations. Signs are posted on the street on either side of every school marking the boundaries of the "drug-free zone."

15. *Arson.* The idea of starting fires to delay classes began in the boys' rooms. Certain students found that if they tossed a match into the receptacle for wastepaper towels, they could get a ten or fifteen minute respite from classes while a fire drill was called and the local fire department put out the blaze.

When ten or fifteen minutes weren't a long enough break, these students decided that the answer was to move on to something more dramatic— like setting the curtains on the stage on fire, or throwing a match into the janitors' supply closet when the door was left unlocked.

In older school buildings, which were not fire-retardant, the entire building was often destroyed, resulting in a two- or three-week vacation for the students while the board of education and administration made temporary plans to house them. Perhaps this was the intent of these students when they made their plans to "torch" the building.

16. *Guns and other Weapons.*

> CLEARWATER—A 16 year old sentenced to six years in state prison for his role in a school cafeteria shooting that killed an assistant principal is anxious to serve his time and get it over with, his mother said.
>
> The boy embraced his mother after his sentencing Friday in the shootings at Pinellas Park High School. He had pleaded guilty to third-degree murder and three counts of burglary with a deadly weapon.

Newspaper accounts such as the one above are not limited to Florida nor to any other state. More and more frequently the public is learning about students who are bringing weapons to school with the intent of using them to inflict an injury or death upon a fellow student or upon a teacher or administrator against whom they have a grudge. In many cases the student goes berserk and shoots wildly into a crowd of students and faculty.

In some inner schools the situation has become so grave that teachers fear for their lives each day they stand before their classes. Metal detectors have been installed in some of these schools, but even with this precaution, guns and other weapons are still smuggled into the building— passed through windows to an accomplice waiting inside.

Evaluation

Rate each of the following statements by placing an x beneath the number which best describes the conditions in your community's school. Then draw a continuous line through the x's to form a graph.

1 2 3 4 5

- Children in the elementary schools in my community are orderly and attentive to teacher-directions while in the hallways.
- Children in the elementary schools in my community are attentive and respectful during assembly programs.
- Children in the elementary schools in my community during lunch time keep their voices at a reasonable level of loudness,

- clean up their tables when they have finished eating, throw all refuse in the trash containers, and do not throw food or other objects.
- At least one certified teacher is on duty during elementary school lunch periods.
- All children in the elementary school in my community engage in meaningful activities during recess.
- I have made observations in the high schools of my community and find:

    That there is no evidence of excessive noise in hallways and other areas of the building.

    That there is no running in the halls.

    That students do not bang lockers as they pass down hallways.

    That students do not roam the halls during periods without a pass and do not disturb classes in session by peering in windows.

    That students do not needlessly set off fire alarms.

    That truancy is at a minimum.

    That fights between students are rare.

- That there is no evidence of drag racing or other violations of the motor vehicle code on school roadways.
- That smoking is not permitted in any school buildings or grounds.
- That boys' and girls' rooms are free of cigarette smoke.
- That there is little evidence of student vandalism throughout the building.
- That there is no evidence of alcohol or drug abuse.
- That theft of school or student property occurs only occasionally.
- That kissing and petting in the school and on the school grounds is not permitted and the rule is strictly enforced.
- That there have been no cases of teen-age sex reported on school property. Teen-age pregnancy is low.
- That there has never been an incidence of arson attributed to a student.
- That there has never been any evidence of students bringing weapons to school.

Chapter Thirteen

THREE HEALTH PROBLEMS

Back in colonial times children attending school had to worry about such possible dangers as Indian attacks or encountering wild animals or poisonous reptiles on their way to and from school.

Today's dangers to school children can't be seen, smelled, tasted, or felt, yet they lurk in many of the nation's schools. Parents should be aware of their existence and should check with school officials to make sure that measures have been taken to protect children from these hidden hazards.

There are three of them which are currently known; how many more there are which haven't as yet been identified is anyone's guess.

Lead in the Water System. Schools built within the last thirty or forty years undoubtedly contain copper pipes which carry the water to various parts of the building. When these pipes were originally installed, they were "sweated" together to make one continuous pipe. Lead-based solder was used in all of these joints and probably within the drinking fountains situated at various places about the building.

Tests have now revealed that as water flows through these joints a minute quantity of the lead in the solder is mixed with the water. The combination of many joints in the expanse of pipe in a large building can build up to dangerous levels by the time it reaches the drinking fountain.

Historians tell us that the elite members of ancient Roman society died at an early age, and for many years no one could understand why. Then, when medical science learned of the deadly effect of lead upon the human system, the answer became clear: only the affluent members of Roman society could afford to purchase dishes and mugs made of lead; the poor ate and drank from dishes and cups made of pottery.

Authorities have also known for a number of years that the lead in paint, when ingested by children, could cause illness and eventually death if consumed over a long period of time. But until recently no one thought much about the possibility that our school's water systems could be contaminated by the discharge of lead into the water from the solder.

Lead-based solder is no longer used in schools or homes; it has been replaced by a silver-based product, more expensive, but safe.

Asbestos. Many schools and other public buildings constructed in the last one hundred years used extensive amounts of asbestos. Schools built during the early part of the century used asbestos as a covering for all pipes which carried steam to the radiators in classrooms.

More modern buildings made use of asbestos as a sound-deadening agent. Auditorium ceilings, particularly, were plastered with an asbestos coating, as were entrance halls and other areas where the architect needed a material that would reduce the sound level when large numbers of people were present.

Pathologists have determined that if a single fiber of asbestos settles in the lungs of an individual it will probably remain there for the remainder of that person's life. They also believe that the individual runs the risk of developing lung cancer.

The most dangerous type of asbestos installation, therefore, is the kind from which particles of the fiber can break loose and become suspended in the air.

Many schools, now aware of the danger of asbestos, have spent millions of dollars to have it removed from their schools. In some cases the risk factor was so great that the buildings were vacated for a full school year while the asbestos was removed.

Radon. Radon is the newcomer to the scene. It has only been a few years since scientists have discovered this odorless, invisible gas and have determined the great potential danger that its presence brings to those who are exposed to it.

Radon is produced when uranium deposits underneath the ground decay. The gas filters up through the soil and enters buildings through minute cracks or around water and sewer pipes. It is particularly dangerous during the winter months when buildings are closed to keep out the cold; during these months the gas can build up within a house or a school until it reaches extremely dangerous levels.

Not all regions of the country are exposed to the dangers of radon gas. Only through tests can a school determine how extensive the peril is. Furthermore, it can vary greatly from classroom to classroom and from one end of a building to another. In two-story buildings the greatest danger is always on the first floor. Buildings that contain basements which have no classrooms are safer than buildings built on a slab.

The U.S. Environmental Protection Agency recently spot-checked 130 school buildings and 3000 classrooms across the country in sixteen states and found that 54 percent of the schools tested had unhealthy levels of radon in at least one room that was occupied by students or staff.

The Environmental Protection Agency considers any level of radon greater than four picocuries per liter of air to be unsafe, and any school building where such measurements have been made should take immediate steps to remedy the problems before students are permitted in the area.

Contrast this with the requirements for companies who employ uranium miners. If radiation levels are sixteen to twenty picocuries per liter of air during continuous work periods, workers are required to wear protective equipment.

At present there are no federal laws which require a school district to test for radon levels, although Congress recently enacted a law obligating the EPA to study the extent of radon contamination in the nation's schools. However the $1.5 million grant for the study has not yet been appropriated.

"These preliminary findings show that radon may be a more serious health problem in our schools than we originally thought—that it may be as serious as asbestos or lead in drinking water," said Senator Quentin Burdick of North Dakota, Chairman of the Senate Environment and Public Works Committee.

Scientists at the EPA have concluded that being exposed to four picocuries of radon is the same as smoking half a pack of cigarettes a day, and that radon is probably responsible for as many as 20,000 lung cancer deaths every year.

Unlike the menace of lead poisoning in the drinking water and asbestos ceilings and asbestos-covered pipes, the elimination of radon in a school is usually a far less expensive an operation.

The use of fan-forced vents to the outside of the building to exhaust the gas from any room where radon has been found is probably the easiest and least complicated remedy. Other methods include sealing off any apertures through the flooring where the gas can enter, placing a plastic barrier beneath the floor, and, in extreme cases, excavating below the room to construct a crawl-space which is then vented to the outside.

Parents should be concerned about the possible presence of these three deadly, unseen dangers which may be affecting their child's future health. The wise parent will not hesitate to check with school officials to learn what measures have been taken by the school to test the level of lead in the school's drinking water, the extent of asbestos in the building and the levels of radon in the air. If these tests have not been made, parents should immediately petition the board of education to make sure that they are conducted by professionals who have the equipment and the know-how to do the job accurately.

And if any of the tests show levels that are dangerous to the occupants of the building, the board of education should be petitioned to close those buildings until they have been made safe.

Evaluation

Rate each of the following statements by placing an x beneath the number which best describes the conditions existing in your community's schools. Then connect the x's with a continuous line to form a graph.

1 2 3 4 5

- All school buildings in my community have been thoroughly examined and have been found to be free of asbestos.
- Any ceilings, pipes or other areas which contained asbestos have been removed and replaced with a nonasbestos covering.
- The water in all the school buildings in my community have been tested for lead and have been certified as being safe to drink.
- Any water systems which tests indicated contained high levels of lead were immediately closed until corrective measures were taken.
- All classrooms and other areas used by students or staff in all school buildings in my community have been tested for radon and have been found to be safe.
- Classrooms which have been found to contain high levels of radon have been kept free of students until protective measures have been taken.

INDEX

189